MAGIC GARDENS

Magic Gardens

A symbolic rendering of angelic communion with man through the medium of flowers.

CORINNE HELINE

Reprint, 1987

NEW AGE BIBLE & PHILOSOPHY CENTER
1139 Lincoln Blvd.
Santa Monica, CA 90403

Dedicated to

MAX HEINDEL

whose
appreciation
and encouragement were
chiefly responsible for
bringing these pages into being.

In Flowerland the whispers of
heaven may become audible to
the children of men; for the
celestial hosts, too, have a way
of "saying it with flowers."

Contents

The talking oak
To the ancient spoke,

But any tree
Will talk to me.

What truths I know
I garnered so.

But those who want to talk and tell,
And those who will not listeners be,
Will never hear a syllable
From out the lips of any tree.

—*Mary Carolyn Davies*

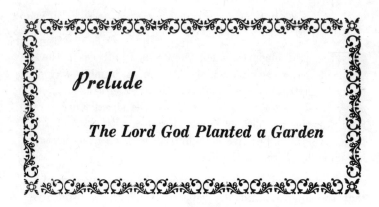

Prelude

The Lord God Planted a Garden

The Lord God planted a garden
In the first white days of the world,
And He set there an angel warden
In a garment of light unfurled.

The kiss of the sun for pardon,
The song of the birds for mirth,
One is nearer God's heart in a garden
Than anywhere else on earth.

—Dorothy Frances Gurney

Every flower bears a starry imprint, declared the illumined seer, Paracelsus. From the zodiac come the veritable secrets of God. The Star Angels are transmitters, and flowers become symbols of their communications. The closer our communion with the angels, the deeper will be our understanding of the mysteries of the plant kingdom and the greater our realization of the spiritual ministry of the world of flowers.

Each of the zodiacal Hierarchies creates its own cosmic flower patterns in the celestial realms. These patterns conform in shape, size, color and tone—every flower sings —with the vibratory keynote of its sign. These cosmic prototypes are perfect in every detail. In the highest heavens they live and bloom in such wondrous beauty as to have inspired many legends which serve in a humble way to bring to earth some slight conception of their transcendent glory in the higher worlds and also the significance they hold for the peoples of earth. Imbued with eternal life they never fade, but live and flourish with an ever-increasing splendor through the ages.

It is from these perfect patterns in the heaven worlds that the angels build the reflections which we who live upon the earth, know as flowers, and which, when so understood, become among the most sublime of earth's teachers. Each flower family is given its own special work to perform. Each plant bears deeply within its heart a message to the human family.

In the earliest stages of their development, flowers, however lovely, were without fragrance, for perfume is the soul of the blossom, and soul is acquired only through service.

Each flower family was fashioned by the angels to represent some specific quality or attribute to be awakened within man. As the angelic hosts impress this ideal upon a floral archetype, its physical embodiment becomes a radiant herald of this celestial message. Flowers are thus literally a medium of contact between the Shining Ones and those who live upon the earth, their fragrance developing and increasing as a beautiful testimony to their work as mediators. As man becomes increasingly sensitive he will begin to interpret this flower language, and to the degree that he does this, and lives in accordance with its high idealism in his daily contacts with his fellowman, the perfume of our flower friends will be intensified, the colorings will grow more exquisite, and the delicate petals will have greater endurance.

Each plant bears in its life forces the signature of its stellar creation. This creative impress takes form within

12

the heart of the seed, and one who possesses the "blessed sight" can observe within it the complete picture of the plant that is later to come into a physical expression upon the earth. So, too, may those possessing the "inner wisdom" discern the message which flowers bring concerning the realities of heaven, and which are awaiting manifestation on the physical plane.

As a man learns to respond to the ideals instilled by the angelic beings into the hearts of flowers, he, too, will develop a quality of soul that will radiate in fragrance, rare and beautiful. He will walk in an aura of radiant light and know the glory of an immortal life that shall never fade.

The Soul's Garden

A garden is a lovesome thing
   God wot!
      Rose plot,
         Fringed pool,
         Ferned grot.
The veriest school of peace;
And yet the fool
Contends that God is not.
Not God! In gardens! when the eve is cool?
Nay, but I have a sign—
'Tis very sure God walks in mine.

—Thomas Edward Brown

Because the physical environment is cramped and limited, and since the soul must have freedom to grow and expand, to study and dream, there come joyous pilgrimages into wider horizons, into more extended fields of exploration, far away, unfettered, free. Across the white page of an infinite scroll the Finger of Truth imprints many indelible lessons. From their high place in the skies these lessons are carried down to earth where they struggle forth into expression, sometimes vague, sometimes distinct, but never of such crystal clarity as they possess on high.

On one of these journeys I saw in the distance something that looked like a great crimson bloodstain on the horizon. Upon coming nearer, I discovered an enormous garden of red roses. From all sides they nodded beautiful heads or extended soft, velvety hands to hold me. Their luxurious hearts emitted a glamorous perfume that enthralled me even though the excess of it was nauseating and repellant. The heavy fragrance of the air was broken only by the whirring of wings, as birds of brilliant plumage sailed by, gloriously colored, but strangely mute.

Despite the radiant coloring that marked this garden it was devoid of all sound. I seemed to feel only a vague undercurrent of restlessness that pervaded all things, and above the revel of color hung a silence, deep and impenetrable.

In the distance walked a maiden, the very spirit of the garden incarnate in all its glowing, passionate beauty. She caressed a cluster of the crimson roses, but they faded very quickly, and as she tossed them from her with a gesture of weariness, they lay shriveled at her feet, strangely like ashes of hopes and broken dreams.

As I longed intensely to know the mystery of this alluring place, a voice emerged out of the silence: "This is the garden of sensual love in all its evanescent, fleeting beauty; it is the garden of the red rose that typifies the love that is human only. Here each soul returns many times and lingers long, straying through this tangled wilderness of crimson beauty. It is only after a protracted journey through tears and shadows that the heart awakens to the realization that the roses which grow here can never become immortal. The glamor of this garden can never be eternal."

Loath to go, yet with an innate urge to leave, I turned away, and as soon as my eyes were clear of the strange lights in the crimson garden, there arose before my vision another enclosure. Here the air was clearer, finer, rarer.

Instead of the disquieting languor of the Red Rose Garden, the very atmosphere was charged with an urging, calling, pleading impulse that pressed upon my soul until it shrank back trembling, afraid to venture further.

This garden was also filled with roses, not crimson as in the other, but of a glowing pink. There were masses of them growing in every conceivable way. Each perfumed depth seemed to hold an insistent appeal toward some higher goal. Innumerable birds lingered here also. They were much lighter in hue than those of the crimson garden and from their musical throats flowed a melodious chorus.

Here, too, wandered a beautiful maiden embodying the very spirit of her surroundings. With smiles on her lips and tender dreams in her eyes, she gathered clusters of roses and held them against her face. Unlike the red roses, these did not quickly wither, but glowed with fresh, pure lights like newly-awakened ideals.

"I could linger here forever," I murmured.

"Yes," answered the voice, "for this is the Garden of Pink Roses; it is the home of aspiration, formed by the mingling of the red rose of human love with the white rose of purity. The soul must live through many life experiences before it can build its sanctuary of purity. Many petals are torn and shattered in the making. Many a rose-builder finds his blossoms bear too deep a crimson hue to live in this garden, and so he must commence again and build anew. But day by day the roses are becoming more beautiful, and the petals are growing more lustrous with newly expressed ideals and aspirations."

Once more I was swept on by an impelling urge toward what appeared like a gleaming star upon the horizon but which, viewed closer, proved to be two gates formed of glowing lights that played back and forth, and between which streamed currents that looked like a shining river. It was the only entrance into another enclosed garden.

17

Awed and silenced, I drew near the gates, when once again the voice whispered, "You cannot enter here. You must first be freed from all the stains of earth."

Oh, the indescribable radiance of this garden. Nothing here but white roses! An infinitude of blossoms melted into a rare harmony of sound; the air was so tremulous with light that it shone before human eyes like dewdrops spun of silver threads. That which would have been but silence to human ears quivered with melody, and each white and perfect blossom breathed its benediction in wordless music.

As a figure of light, the white Spirit of the Garden, bearing one of the perfect flowers, approached the gates near which she paused and spoke thus: "This white rose is immortal; it is the ideal of soul attainment. Each spirit must build its own individual gates of light, and in the shining of that light discover within itself the glory of its own White Rose Garden, the inner place of peace. Pray— meditate—understand—achieve."

Reluctantly I was dragged back into earth-ways again. Opening wide my window to greet the morning sun, a red rose, a pink rose, and a white rose nodded to me from the garden below, while a little bird sang in a tree nearby.

18

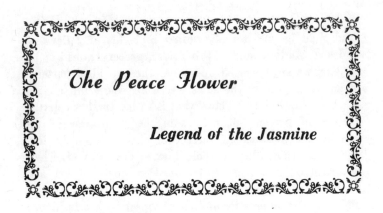

The Peace Flower

Legend of the Jasmine

"Oh that the nations had planted a rose
Instead of a shell in the path of its foes."

Angels hold converse with each other and with mortals by means of color. An assemblage of angels when engaged in healing prayers for the bestowal of blessings upon humanity appear as a glory of variegated clouds that fleck the sky in the hours of dawn or at sunset time.

On particular days which have been set aside as national holidays in commemoration of those who have laid down their lives upon the battlefields of their country, the angels who work most intimately with man are particularly active in broadcasting thoughts and prayers for peace throughout the world. Within each receptive heart they instill this ideal, and in every receptive mind they impress its noble impulse and power. The angels are assisted in this work by those on earth who have unselfishly laid their lives upon the altar of sacrifice for their country's good.

White is the light that suffuses a land when observing nationally the sacred memory of its war-time dead. Above the tall marble shafts that rise so proudly toward the blue, and beneath which sleep the honored dead, the angels hover in mighty companies of peace. Their chorals are of the time when war shall be no more. They sing of the coming day of brotherhood when the hearts of all man-

kind shall be indissolubly united in bonds of fellowship
and love. As they sing of this nobler, peaceful world to be,
its likeness is impressed upon the ethers in ideal patterns
which sweep across the skies where all whose inner sight
is active may see and know what is to be. In that celestial
picture of promise may be seen the joyousness of the
people, the radiance of their countenances and the love
and trust which they all hold toward one another. Their
beautiful domiciles are emblazoned in works of art and
overhung with clusters of fruits and flowers. Slender spires
gleaming like silhouettes of ancient tapestries are fashioned
amid the stars. It is a realm of eternal loveliness, a land
which can never be despoiled by shrapnel nor bomb. Its
gates are always open wide for whomsoever wills to enter
in and taste of that wondrous peace which passeth all
understanding.

It was such a picture as this that the prophet Isaiah
looked upon when he wrote: "They shall beat their swords
into ploughshares, and their spears into pruning hooks; nation shall not lift up sword against nation, neither shall
they learn war any more. —They shall not hurt nor destroy
in all my holy mountain; for the earth shall be full of the
knowledge of God, as the waters cover the sea."

The angels, too, seem transported in joy with the
divine beauty of this ideal which they fashion above the
earth and which by the power and rhythm of their celestial songs they seem to build into the very souls of men. So
powerful are their radiations and so intense the rhythms,
that all the earth is beginning to sense the meaning of a
world-wide peace.

Winging through the vast ethereal expanses, hosts of
angels gather some of the fairest, whitest and most fragrant blossoms which adorn their etheric Land of Eternal
Peace. These flowers they bring to the dust-haunted aisles
of earth. They are of ethereal whiteness and celestial sweetness, for of all flowers the Jasmine is most fragrant.

The snowy whiteness of the Jasmine-flower reflects the divine peace; its fragrance, the prayers of angels. From the heart of this blossom, streamers of good-will ray out to all the world; from its petals are broadcast the powers of peace.

During the silent hours of the night when stars alone watch over the white sepulchral cities built to the memory of those who have died for the betterment of man, angels often pause to sing of the coming day when these silent acres shall be no more. It is then that the fragrance of the Jasmine, the peace flower, broods in a white, healing magic above the heart of the sleeping world.

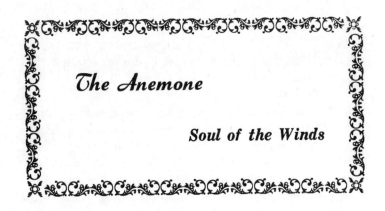

The Anemone

Soul of the Winds

Teach me the secret of thy loveliness,
That being wise I may aspire to be
As beautiful in thought, and so express
Immortal truths to earth's mortality.
Though, too, my soul's ability be less
Than 'tis to thee, O sweet anemone.

                                    —*Madison Cawein*

The more spiritual a people become, the more completely does every object of their outer knowing correspond symbolically to their inner life and to the unfoldment of their spiritual powers. Thus it is that the Flower Kingdom reflects qualities in man with whom they are in truth related in a deeper sense than is generally recognized. Flowers are a veritable Book inscribed with Signatures of the Soul. In them are expressed the finer elements of man's nature.

Flowers that sleep in the heart of Mother Earth during the long months of frost and snow and reawaken with the coming of the spring-tide forces, clothing all nature in new robes of verdure and color, are fitting symbols of that innate divinity sleeping within the heart of every man which, when awakened, causes him to put off the old man and to put on the new.

It was the understanding of this mystic illumination that animated the ecstatic soul-song of Isaiah: "Arise and sing ye that dwell in the dust, for thy dew is as the dew of herbs." St. Paul made reference to this same transfiguring process when he wrote: "Ye shall not all die, but ye shall all be changed."

To commemorate this wondrous transforming process in the life of man, the angels have fashioned a flower. That flower is formed of the sweetness and the perfume of the winds, and sheds its fragrant beauty upon the world in the gladsome Resurrection Season.

The Anemone, flower of the transformed, is shrouded in all the mystery of that early time when angels walked with men and instructed them in the lore of the celestial sciences. Adonis, according to the ancient legend, was the beloved of the goddess Venus. When in death the blood flowed from his wounds, as it touched the earth, it mingled with the grieving tears of Venus, and behold! there sprang up in miracle the Anemone, the lovely fragile flower of the winds.

Within the blood lies the mystery of the transforming processes in man, the keynote of which is purity. The body of an Illuminated One is always adorned with flowers, or interior stars. These are centers of light or magnets of spiritual force. Thus the Anemone is representative of that force fashioned within man's own holy temple through the redemptive power of love, or the goddess Venus of the ancient legend.

For a day the Anemone bears the message of this wondrous soul miracle to earth, and then its tenuous petals close and the spirit of its beauty is wafted back into heaven, there to add new vibrancy and meaning to the song of the angels concerning the future emancipation of man.

> *But be thy blood a flower*
> *. . . For such a change?*
> *From thence a flower, alike in color rose*
> *Such as those trees produce, whose fruits enclose*
> *Within the limber rind their purple grains.*
> *—Ovid.*

24

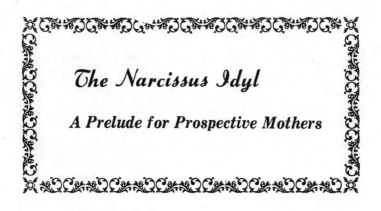

The Narcissus Idyl

A Prelude for Prospective Mothers

It looked
As if the water were alive.
Himself,
In love with his own self lay there unmoved
Of gaze, like Parian marble statuesque;
And saw, as in a mirror, the two sweet eyes,
His own reflection, as it might be stars.
                                        —Ovid.

I

Many of the fables of antiquity are founded on the Secret Mysteries. The Greeks recount a legend of the woodland nymph Narcissus, who, when gazing upon his mirrored likeness in the water of a crystal pool, became enamored of his own beautiful reflection. This mystic water was always strangely still, and it had the appearance of molten silver. To this quiet place the shepherds never drove their flocks, nor did any mountain beast come near it; neither was it defaced with fallen leaves or branches.

Water is a symbol of the etheric or reflecting plane of nature. All spiritual truths are mirrored in this silvery silent water, and he who is sufficiently wise, whether he be on this earth sphere or in the higher realms, may read these gleaming pages. It is here that tenuous lines of light

25

like tangled skeins, mark the contact of soul with soul, and keep intact the patterns set in many life encounters of the past.

Narcissus, the radiant youth, is one who has learned to read this mystic scroll, visible alone to sight grown impersonal. As Narcissus became enamored with his beautiful personality, his tears fell in the water and disturbed the image. Eyes that still remain channels for tears cannot discern the lettering on these fair pages. It is here that egos coming into earth life find their rightful place, and where mothers who are sufficiently wise may meet and know their own.

For love of self, Narcissus lost his radiant beauty (his spiritual contacts), and when he died, there was woeful lamentation among the water nymphs. Love of the personality it is that ever causes these shoreless waters to mist in oblivion. The body of Narcissus faded away, but in his memory the angels set upon the banks of this silver pool a flower which bears his name, and which in its radiance and perfumed fairness carries the impress of his story.

> *On the greensward he laid a weary head,*
> *Death closed the eyes that loved their owner's charm*
> *No corse was anywhere, they a flower found,*
> *Yellow at heart, with snow-white petals round.*
>
> —*Ovid*

"The visible is fleeting, the invisible is eternal. Heaven is reflected upon earth." Thus do the angels speak in the magic beauty of the Narcissus blossoms.

II

"Men are what their mothers make them. When each comes forth from his mother's womb the gate of gifts closes behind him."

—*Emerson*

The broad colonnades of a rambling, old portico gleam soft and white in the deepening violet-grey dusk. The house speaks in low, hushed tones of mystery and breathes of rose-hued romance. Tendrils of fragrant vines cling gently about the great porch and form a fret-work with the blue sky through which evening stars gleam like silver candles.

A young woman sits lost in the never-ceasing wonders of the approaching dusk. This is her favorite hour of the day. Always the twilight brings the ecstasy of dreams. For her the night is some great black bird which with soft downy feathers covers the heart of the day and lulls it to rest. Airy fancies flit through her mind like half-sung melodies played upon weary strings. From childhood it has been thus. She has been ever striving to find the soul of some rare truth which always eludes her, leaving only a shadow of vague dissatisfaction that yet is tinged with some strange exaltation.

"Oh, how I hope," she mused, "that the little one who is coming to me soon will gather up the ravelled skeins of life that I have dropped, and untangle them; I hope for one who will be able to find and to give to the world in some way the inner meanings of things which I divine, and of which I know the outer form is but a mere symbol— something that shall be a lasting addition to the beauty and to the truth of the world."

So she dreamed, and her dreams were fragrant with longing as the shadows fell, and the brooding black bird of night nestled softly about the heart of day crooning a slumber-song of exceeding sweetness.

In the realms of the unborn an ego eagerly awaits return to earth again. High dreams of becoming a famous artist had animated the previous earth-life. But these dreams had not been realized. Obstacles, one after another, had frustrated his ambitions. Yet all had not been lost. From difficulties and disappointments he had learned to

27

bear bravely the cross of defeat and the crown of hopeless aspirations.

During the time of preparation for rebirth in the higher realms, this soul had worked to find the reason for his failure so that he might now build anew upon better foundations than in the past. Receiving the call to another earth life he joyously answered it. The music in his artist-soul responded to this prospective mother's yearning dreams. Holding the colors of the higher realms ever in his consciousness, he went forth once again with high hope and noble purpose to bring his ideals to earthly fruition.

III

The afternoon sun poured through the casement, flooding the gorgeous apartment with a mellow, golden light. The room was large and magnificently furnished. Rare tapestries and art-treasures from many parts of the world adorned it, evincing cultivated taste and great wealth.

Beside the open window sat the mistress of this rich domain, a woman young and fair. Her eyes, wandering over her beautiful possessions, sparkled with pleasure, her color heightened, and her whole attitude bespoke exultation as she thought of the child with whom she would soon be able to share these wordly treasures. Presently she was to receive into her keeping a soul who was undertaking another pilgrimage in earthly form.

Proudly she hopes for a son, and many are the plans she makes for his life. Her social position and unlimited wealth will give him opportunities possessed by few. She thinks and plans, ambition being her constant companion as the days lengthen into the weeks in which she is helping to build the earth-house for its new tenant.

The chords of her ambition stretch away into the plane where souls are awaiting rebirth; in that realm they call forth a response from an ego of like disposition whose eagerness to return to earth life is as strong as is the desire of this expectant mother to provide the opportunity.

An ego strongly drawn by earth desires has longed for the world 'of form and the opportunities which it offers for exercising the added faculties gained during the interval of waiting between earth lives. By the law of attraction the worldly desires and ambitions of the mother-to-be and the ego awaiting incarnation, drew the two into even closer union until each found fulfillment in the other.

IV

Again a woman, young and fair, is thinking of the time when a soul is to be entrusted into her keeping. But there are no hopes of high ambitions, no dreaming fancies; only the plain matter-of-fact life of every day. Her thoughts wander not beyond the present, or if they do she brings them back sharply. "What is the use of wasting time with fancy conjecture?" she asks herself. "This present life is all we know for certainty. Our five senses can give us no more. I shall be satisfied with this life, and take it as I find it, leaving all fanciful speculations to those who have the time to indulge in them."

So she lived her life day by day, quite unaware that a mother by her thoughts, her dreams, and her aspirations is shaping the character, condition and the soul atmosphere in which an incoming ego takes form.

Of the many spirits waiting a return to earth life there are none for whom the inner planes hold so much tedium and monotony as for the materialist. Having failed to recognize the reality of the spiritual world, he has blinded his own consciousness to its existence. Having, furthermore, made no preparation for life after death, he goes out blinded and empty handed and with little or nothing to work upon while in the inner world. Thus this interval becomes a period of tiresome waiting for return to another physical experience.

An ego who has waited through this dreary interval of time receives the bidding from an expectant mother with gladness. Thus the woman who has closed her eyes to the light of spiritual things opens the door of her heart to welcome this entering soul.

V

The reincarnating ego, in preparing for the work of the coming earth life, is over-shadowed and permeated by the Universal Spirit. This same over-brooding and protecting Spirit finds most sublime manifestation on earth in mother love. The spiritually minded mother is attuned to the Cosmic Feminine Principle and cooperates understandingly with the universal Law of Life and Love. It is the mothers who are to become the torch bearers of the New Race.

The expectant New Age mother, living on the mountain tops of thought, often experiences ecstasies that almost over-awe even her pure soul with their indescribable loveliness. Enveloped in the radiance of the spirit with whom she is consciously working and for whom she is fashioning a new body, she becomes a light to all prospective mothers by which they may see more clearly the divine privilege which is theirs when giving prenatal bent to an incoming soul. By attuning her thoughts and her life to the good, the beautiful, and the true, she makes of these a mystic garment which she wraps about her and the incoming ego with whom she is bound by ties from other lives. On glad wings the day is approaching when every woman shall kneel before this shrine of Truth and so win for her brow a crown of eternal immortelles.

VI

The old house still breathes of sweet rose-hued romance and whispers mysterious messages from the past. The little Weaver of Dreams still sits behind the white colonnades and watches the darkening world. As always, she revels in the mystery and the beauty of life.

The one who came to her in the years agone is now a master of color. His pictures are living poems. He seems to have caught all her airy fancies and to have woven them into a harmony of lights and shadows more ethereal than any the world has ever known. They are quivering echoes of music that have been hushed only to sing on in tones of color. They hold the light of strange fires, a touch of the heart's blood, a perfume of immortal flowers, an inner sacred beauty of the soul. To this mother there now comes the added happiness of realizing that she had used her own artistic faculties in aiding the ego who became her son. By living her ideal every day, she had so impregnated her consciousness with its truth, that all unaware she opened the gate of gifts for a wonderful Spirit to come into his own.

VII

A woman with silver-gray hair and a face on which disappointment has drawn many lines sits beside the window of a magnificent apartment. As her eyes wander over the treasures before her, she thinks sorrowfully of the past and recalls how many years ago beside that same window she had planned such a brilliant future for the son who was to be hers. With an aching heart she reviews his youth so filled with promise.

She remembers even now that with the passing of the years his ambitions seemed to grow insatiable. He fulfilled the plans she had for him—and more. However, his life was so filled with worldly dreams to be realized, with the amassing of more wealth for their already swollen treasury and the attainment of a higher social position, that he had no time or thought for love or mother. Recently he had succumbed to a brief illness in a foreign land.

"What is the use?" she moaned to her heart. "After all my ambitions were realized, what did they give me? I

had planned so long before he came to me. He more than
fulfilled my greatest hopes of earthly glory. Yet where is
the happiness? I am prone to believe that the seeker of
worldly attainment is, after all, merely a chaser of rainbows. I would that I could live my life over again.''
The tears fell on her wan face. And far away tears of
raindrops fell on the new-made grave and echoed, ''A
chaser of rainbows.''

VIII

A mother who had boasted of her sound logic, her
common sense and of always having her ''feet on the
ground'' sat watching with eyes of adoration a slender girl
who reclined upon the couch. By her movements one can
perceive that she is blind. Suddenly the girl exclaimed:
''Mother, it is not such a terrible misfortune to be physi-
cally blind when one can see such wonderful inner lights as
I do. They are so brilliant, so dazzling, and they all seem
to be dancing. Sometimes I hear the strangest, floating
music and yet it all seems to be inside of me. I can't describe it, but at such times I am not conscious that I have
a physical body at all. I seem to live in mid-air. We have
grieved together so often over my infirmity, and now such
a strange thought has come to me, mother dear; maybe I
did live another life somewhere, and perhaps I was then
as you are now, skeptical concerning all things that could
not be proven by the five senses, and bitterly denounced
as you do now, all those who held other beliefs. So because
I was blind to spiritual things then, and possibly withheld
the light from others, the Law has caused me to be physi-
cally blind now. There is part of me that still wants to
believe your materialistic theories, but Oh, my mother,
when these wonderful experiences come to me, then to
doubt is futile, *I know.*''

With lives that are dedicated to working together for
the highest, with hearts over-flowing with love for humanity, and with souls fragrant with the aroma of good
deeds, the spiritually awakened mother and the wise one
to whom she gave fitting embodiment, are approaching the
evening of their earthly activity. Life has been for them
a glad song of service, a symphony of aspiration and
idealism in which the softened, shadowed earth-tones by
day blend with the triumphant overtones of night. Their
lives have united the conscious realization of Invisible
Helpership with their beautiful ministry of the day. They
hold the key which opens the gate of gifts for egos awaiting an opportunity for new earth experiences. They have
found the light pointing toward the new day of awakened
motherhood, when a greater understanding will enable en-
lightened ones to live and work in perfect harmony with
Cosmic Law.

Mothers will then in recognition of the sacred time
when they are preparing a new body-temple for an incar-
nating spirit, ascend with the blessed Mary into the hill
country of consciousness, there to meet and claim their
own.

Soul Remembrance

The Rosemary Legend

There's rosemary—that's for remembrance.
—Shakespeare

Two souls there are who often walk together along the highways of life. One of these two is clothed in the light of the morning and wears the beauty of the sunrise. He radiates the gladness of spring, the joy of creation. His breath is the perfume of flowers and his voice the music of hope in the heart of youth.

As he draws his bow of light across a magic violin vibrant with harmony, the joyous music transfigures the face of all nature and re-echoes through infinite space. A soft light mellows the landscape, the sea shimmers in a gentle cadence; and flowers bend beneath the radiance of a new beauty. Everything is transformed. The whole world sings a paean of joy.

The youthful musician flourishes his bow with peals of laughter: "See how earth and air and sky obey me? Wherever I go, all is mine. The beautful becomes more beautiful at my touch; the fair infinitely fairer. I am the soul of all things for I am the Soul of Joy."

Another, attracted by the power of the musician, draws near and approaches him with outstretched arms. The companion of the Soul of Joy has remained motionless during the spell cast by the entrancing music. His gaze holds the mystery of far visions, and his face, the sorrow of deep knowledge. There is a perfume of strange flowers about him, flowers that have grown in solitudes on wind-swept heights amid eternal snows.

In the deepening silence he draws his violin close to his heart and begins to play. First there is a note of tender wailing that seems drawn from the very heart strings, gradually merging into a plaintive sobbing chant. Finally it changes into a wild tempest of agony that eventually ends in a tremolo of resignation.

The face of nature changes in unison with the moods of the violin. Winds sob through the trees, banks of flying clouds obscure the moon, the waves of the sea fall upon the shore like the agonized beating of some great wounded heart. As the music fades into the silence, a strange un-earthly beauty envelops the night. The clouds disappear against the blue-black sky. Over rough, stony ways spring flowers not planted by human hands. The sea croons a slumber-song wrapped in a moonlight fairer than any mortals know. Everywhere flowers are blooming in a tender, yearning beauty that is lustrous with a sheen resembling tears.

As this strange music passes into other realms, the unearthly beauty of the night envelops the musician. He stands, a living flame quivering with unutterable longings, unexpressed desires, unfathomed truths. He turns to the Soul of Joy who is transfixed with wonderment.

"You say you make the beautiful more beautiful, the fair, infinitely fairer. You ever create; you build anew. But I resurrect, I transmute. The barren I make beautiful. The hideous, the ill-formed, I translate into a new life. I find beauty where before it was not; I wring peace from the depths and cause it to live upon the heights. I bring perfection, completion. Even you, Oh Soul of Joy, can never be known in your innermost self without me, for I am the Soul of Pain."

36

The one who had stood so close to the Soul of Joy now turns and goes forward eagerly to meet this strange Being, a new light dawning in his eyes. The Soul of Pain reaches out his hands in tender benediction saying: "Oh Spirit of Man, I bless you."

—:—

In the deep silence of the soul, sleep many forgotten secrets that the Spirit knew before it bound itself within these blinding veils of flesh, high white yearnings which it intuitively gropes for in its profound moments, and which in such moments flash out as vague memories of some far-off time.

Before spirits leave their celestial abode for another period of experience in the shadow-land of earth, un-dimmed is the vision and clear is this higher knowing. It is only the robe of mortality which obscures the knowledge of life's true values and causes the ceaseless, restless searchings which lead to disillusionment and pain. The angels are sad because of this mortal blindness, and so deep in the heart of one of their love-blossoms they have buried a song that goes something like this:

"Life is made not for pleasure, but for experience. Whether its deepest notes sound in gladness or in tears, the soul that bears the richest legacy on its return to God is the one who has lived to the full every moment of life, extracting to the utmost the essence of its experience and building it into the gold of its shining aura."

Thus sings the little Rosemary, the flower of remembrance, for all who will pause and be still long enough to hear its song. "It is only one who has found the tears that gleam in the heart of every joy and the ecstasy which broods within the light of every sorrow who is wise enough to listen to the song of the Rosemary and *remember*." Thus the angels chant as they breathe a perfumed blessing upon its starry petals.

37

A Divine Adventure

With a Daffodil and the Sea

I wandered down a lane of golden light,
And found a dell unspoiled, by man untrod,
And with the daffodil for acolyte
I bared my soul to all the woods—and God.

—Stephen Maylau Bird

One day as I wandered by the sea, symbol of that brooding, mothering Oversoul into which I pour all my fancies and which gives back to me dreams so rare that I grope for words to give them expression, I was reading a group of strangely beautiful poems on rebirth and seemed just on the verge of remembrance. The sea called with strange and insistent music, "Don't you remember? Don't you remember? Come closer. Bend lower. Let me take your hand and waft you away beyond physical limitations through vast yesterdays and over infinite horizons into vistas of tomorrow. A wonderful power is mine which shall one day also be yours to command."

The sole companion of my dreaming was a perfect flower that nestled close and seemed to palpitate in sympathy with my deep love for the sea. As I gazed into its radiant heart it gave back to me mystical, unutterable musings in its perfume.

While I read and pondered, I decided to let my flower-companion dream on the heart of a quiet pool drowsing among the rocks. Soon my outer consciousness was rapt in following the adventures of a soul for whom death and birth were no longer a sleep and a forgetting. Suddenly the incoming tide swept across the rocks and carried my little flower out to sea. I ran down the beach but to no avail. Three high breakers rolled over it. As each one caught it up, the tiny petals crumpled as with pain. All unheeded the tears came, and I hold out my arms with a cry: "O my beloved sea! How could you? How could you? When I love you so."

Something just then bade me turn and watch the sun sinking behind hills that were shimmering like great heaps of crushed rose leaves sifted through beds of violets. Wonderfully comforted, as always, by coming close to the beautiful, I turned away. Glancing toward the pool nestling among the rocks I saw there an idly drifting object. Going closer I fell to my knees in the sand, for there lay my flower, without a stain or bruise, as sweet and fair as though it had nestled undisturbed in the heart of some quiet garden. I held out my arms with a glad cry of thankfulness to my beloved sea.

The answer came in resonant, blue whirls of laughter: "Don't you remember? Don't you remember? Come closer. Bend lower. Let me take you by the hand and waft you away over infinite horizons into vistas of tomorrow. A wonderful power is mine which shall one day also be yours to command."

A Legend of the Heliotrope

Children of too gentle birth,
Here these flowers lie,
Love that never quite touched earth,
They — and thou and I.

—B. R. C. Low

Upon the broad shining highway of Life a Woman's soul stands musing. On her arm she bears a basket filled with bundles, and upon these she fixes her eyes thoughtfully. After a long time she lifts one that shines with a strange brightness; upon it is inscribed; "What the World Knows as Love." She unfolds it carefully and regards for awhile its tawdry glory, after which she lays it aside saying sadly, "Nothing but tinsel, nothing but tinsel." She chooses another that glows with a flickering light, sometimes giving out a brilliant radiance, and again on closer scrutiny emitting only a pale gleam. This one is marked "Ambition." After a time she puts this, too, aside with a weary sigh and looks long and earnestly upon the remaining contents of the basket. Finally she chooses one that lies close to the bottom. This is labeled, "Worldly Possessions." Regarding it eagerly for a time she sees it, too, beginning to crumble and fade. "Ashes and dead sea fruit," she murmurs bitterly, casting it away.

She opens another that is well-worn and looks as though it has been much handled. This one is called "Fame." It is cold to the touch, so she tries to warm it by laying it against her heart. Finding no response she turns away saying, "There is no happiness here, I must look further." Half shrinking, yet wonderingly, she unbinds the wrappings of soft grey and mauve that cling close around the last of the bundles. Upon this is engraved, "Death." While she examines it curiously there comes dancing in front of her what appears to be a fairy bubble, all flowing with a rare light that does not seem to belong to earth. One moment it hovers close above her head; then as she strives to reach it, it floats away into the blue ethers; but always when about to vanish it swerves gracefully and comes close to earth again, lighting the shining highway of Life for a long way wherever its shadow is cast.

As its light falls upon her, the grey bundle in her hands melts away. "My dream of love that the angels have given me," the woman's soul cries softly. "The love that outlives aeons of time and the vast cycle of lives; the real love of soul for soul that in its idealism and purity knows no limitations and transmutes even death itself into life."

She slips to her knees in adoration as the strange new light breaks over her, encircling her with wave after wave of almost heavenly splendor.

In the region where angels await prayerfully the decisions of a woman's soul, there sounds a chant of praise and thanksgiving. To commemorate the coming of this new ideal into the world they have caused a flower to be born. So feathery are its blossoms that they scarce can bear the light of day, for the flower can be no stronger than the conception which has given it birth. Blue is the color of spiritual love, so blue is the color tone in which this flower, fresh from the heaven world, whispers its message to woman's soul. So fragile are the petals that it is as though angels have just loaned them to humanity as a promise or harbinger of a dream not yet fully realized. At present the blossoms in all their perfect beauty can live in the atmosphere of earth for only a little time; beneath human thought and touch they soon shrivel and blacken, and leave only a fleeting memory of the ideal they symbolize.

As the beauty and purity of the message which this little flower holds in the purple fragrance of its heart becomes more deeply implanted in woman's soul, and as the holy conception from which it was born sheds its blessing across the world, this tiny messenger of the angels, this most ethereal of all flowers, will gradually lose its tenuous fragility and gladden for a longer time the hearts of those who have learned to read its meaning in the perfect beauty of its blossoming.

The Golden Amaranth

Their crown inwove with amaranth and gold;
Immortal amaranth, a flower which once
In Paradise fast by the tree of life
Began to bloom.

—*Milton*

When the earth call sounds in heaven, multitudes of white spirits are gathered together by the guardian angels, and those who are ready for a new human experience are prepared to respond to the summons.

In their heaven world state of consciousness, egos know that goodness and truth, life and love, are immortal. As each soul finds its place in the long processional descending to walk earth's ways again, the radiance of this inner knowing, untrammeled by flesh, spreads afar until the multitudes appear transformed into a glory as of descending fires.

A mighty angel stands before the outer confines of the earth-plane holding in his hands a starry cup that flashes and sparkles, as if set with the brightest suns of the skies. Woven about this cup is a fair flower which bears the name of amaranth, meaning ''undying,'' or ''immortal.''

Each returning spirit, as it passes behind the veils of mortality, partakes of this cup, and as it drinks, the angel places within its hand one of these fragile, golden flowers.

45

This is the Cup of Forgetfulness, the cup which causes man to cease to remember that there is no death. All is life. The soul is immortal, and each earth span is but a page in the book of life. Only by reference to the whole of that book can the meaning of life's manifold experiences be reasonably interpreted and adequately understood. But since there is much contained in past pages that we are not yet strong enough to read with equanimity, it is well that all is not remembered. Therefore it is that some who grasp these inner truths have called this cup the Potion of Compassion and the angel who bears it, the Messenger of Charity.

To every incoming ego this beneficent angel gives a golden flower of immortality to serve as a reminder of life eternal so that this high truth may never be forgotten. Some few have kept this little flower close within their hearts where it lives and blossoms in perpetual beauty. These are the teachers of men who go about over the world proclaiming spiritual truths to all who will listen. But the greater number have lost their precious flower and stumble blindly along the highways of earth-life, the spirit groping uncertainly, ever longing to recover its lost and priceless heritage of knowledge.

The Greeks, possessing as they did much inner-world understanding, crowned their heroes and their dead with an amaranthine chaplet as a symbol of the eventual recovery by all men of this inner wisdom.

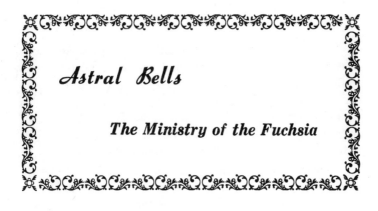

Astral Bells

The Ministry of the Fuchsia

Much have I travelled in realms of gold.
                                    —Keats

The little flowers that "write music in the air."

In the white silences of heaven there is no line of demarcation between day and night; all things and all beings are continuously suffused with a luminous golden glow that knows no surcease nor retardation. However, when the shadows lengthen upon the earth the

> *"Tall oaks' branches charmed by the earnest stars,*
> *Dream, and so dream all night without a stir."*

A quiet hush falls about the courts of heaven; the angels sing more sweetly, and the music of their moving seems to breathe in softer cadences. This is the only signal in that bright land which indicates that the darkness of night has descended upon the earth.

From out this softened silence there peals at certain intervals the chiming music of bells, music that may sometimes be heard even upon earth by those who listen for their ringing. These bells sound at certain specific times when the heart-beat of earth is most closely attuned to the heart of heaven. These hours mortals know as midnight and as dawn.

The astral bells sound the call for troops of spirits to fare forth on errands of Love and mercy for all those who suffer, and for others who have earned the privilege through such serving to ascend into the spiritual realms to receive instruction from the angels. Truly has the poet voiced this vision when referring to ''the great world's altar stairs that slope through darkness up to God.''

Those who have heard the music of these bells are always conscious of the ethereal melody sounding forever within their hearts; with ease does the soul rise in ecstasy in response to the memory it calls forth.

The angels also love to listen to this music of fairy bells, and in the rhythm of its measures they have fashioned a flower that catches the echo and scatters it abroad again upon the world. Fuchsia blossoms are the angelic replica of these astral bells. Just at midnight and at dawn they grow tremulous with melody; the delicate petals bend beneath the inflow of harmony, and the tender pistils sway rhythmically as they re-echo in soft music the ringing of these celestial chimes.

Certain groups of angels there are who work exclusively with the plant kingdom; they permeate the seed with the ethers of life so that the powers sleeping within may awaken in response to the forces of mother earth. Tenderly they mould leaf, petal, stamen and pistil; softly they color each delicate vein as they fashion minute and intricate patterns of rare loveliness and grace. Mortals would be more guarded in handling these rare gifts of the angels could they observe the reverent love and care bestowed upon their formation.

The angels grow very sad before the sorry sight of man's thoughtless and willful mutilation of their precious flower-children, and so when the little Fuchsia Bells peal forth upon the earth an echo of the sweet astral chimes of heaven, troops of flower-angels fly abroad over the world and gather the blossoms which have been bruised and torn, or cast idly aside by the heedless and the uncomprehending to wither and to die. After impressing a blessing upon the tired, fragile, physical forms, the angels tenderly withdraw the life essences and bear them like sweeping gossamer ribbons back into the heavens, there to be used again in their gentle ministries of building other flower patterns with which to bless and beautify man's terrestial home.

The time is not far distant when science will verify these truths sufficiently for every one to understand something of the pain and joy experienced by the inhabitants of the Flower World.

> *And 'tis my faith that every flower*
> *Enjoys the air it breathes.*

So sings Wordsworth, high priest among the flower poets. But unheeded are his words save by the few who with "blessed sight" have perceived something of the angelic ministry in their workings with plant life.

Meanwhile the little Fuchsia Bells sound a call at midnight and at dawn, summoning the angels of mercy to minister to all that grieve and suffer throughout the far-flung realms of Flowerland.

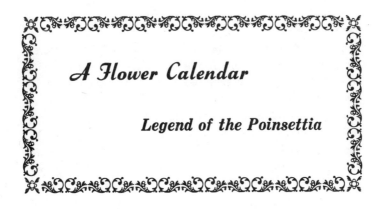

A Flower Calendar

Legend of the Poinsettia

When they have deeply quaffed
From the brimming cups of dew,
You can hear their golden laughter
All the garden through.

—Clinton Scollard

In the years agone, when man walked on earth hand in hand with the angels, knowing only their stainless innocence and radiating only their perfect beauty, and when never a thought of evil had tinged his consciousness and projected its shadows in the outer environment, flowers being reflections of consciousness, all shone in purest white, making the world a veritable dream-garden of pure and fragrant beauty.

As ages passed and the vibrations of a mighty Star opened the portals of matter for the entrance of man, and spirit became more firmly enmeshed in its material form, the delicately sensitive petals gradually caught and held the colors given to them by the varied thoughts and emotions of men, and only the rarest and finest of the flower-souls were able to blossom in all their former pristine purity.

But for yet a long time there grew a flower so white that it rivaled the breath of mountain snows; the neck of the swan was pale beside it. Tradition holds that wherever a pure soul lived unspotted by the world these flowers blossomed in profusion. Along pathways steeped in meditations of saints they shone as fair as the thoughts which they reflected.

On the first Holy Night, when shepherds were watching upon the Judean hills, and the golden Star guided them on their way to the sacred manger, their path was strewn with these white mystic blossoms, which the rays from the Star of the East turned into shimmering silver.

When the Holy One carried the cross up the steep ascent of Golgotha, the ground was carpeted white with their beauty. They clustered lovingly about His bruised feet as though they would fain make amends for the cruel nails and the crown of thorns. Silently their white faces watched in mute appeal the enactment of the crucifixion. The fragile petals shivered in sympathy with the cosmic tremblings that occurred when the Master Spirit broke his bondage of flesh.

As the blood flowed from the piercing nails and the clasp of thorns, one sacred drop fell deep into the heart of a little white blossom. There it nestled. Almost imperceptibly the petals bent low beneath the honor; then softly, gently they flamed into crimson. All through the heart of the earth this force was felt with the result that wherever these mystic flowers bloomed they were changed from pure white into blood red.

The purest soul of all the flower-world through the ages must bathe its heart in the blood of the Christ and give to the world its message through the beauty of flaming petals.

I

The closing time of the flower-year is come, and each petal month has been blown into fragrant sheaves of memory. The Weavers of Flowerland sit in council to decide which blossom shall be held sacred to Christmas.

What flower is fair enough to represent the month of Cosmic Birth? On silken pinions of wind, messages have gone to the Guardian Deities of the months asking them to come and present their claims before the council of the Flower World.

Crooning the slumber song of winter in faint notes of flickering sunlight comes pale January clad in sable garments. Her snow-white arms are laden with fragile hyacinth bells that tremble in soft music to the yearning song her soul must ever sing of Silence and of Sleep.

Toward the short days' end, across the western edge of a low, dark sky, February draws a line of gold, while from the earth's grey heart she gathers tear drops, transmuting them into golden daffodils of promise for the weary world. Miracles she brings to land and sky, for her name of names is Hope.

March wraps the earth in veils of vague and tender greens, and stands with clasped and eager hands while the world-soul plays the prelude of resurrected life. Violets as blue as the sky toward which they left their eyes, spring from her thoughts, for the inner name of March is Aspiration.

Virgin April, clad in shimmering tears, bends above the tired world. Gathering up its pain and sorrows, she presses lily-lips upon them. When they are filled with a holy consciousness of peace, she fashions them into the sweetness of the lily, and commissions them to breathe upon humanity the secret of her soul—Attainment.

May, with lilting laughter, whispers deep into the heart of the woodland, causing it to open the doors of its treasure-house to her. Then she wraps herself in fairy garlands to awaken the spirit of beauty. For May is the soul of Harmony that brings to life the latent beauties of all the Flower World.

Young June, the Soul of Love, in an ecstatic music of dreams, dips her brush in the pigments of the sky, in the crimson of dusk, in the white mists of dawn, in the rose-blush of sunrise and in the amber of gloaming hours. She adds to these the smooth luster of starlight and the sweet breath of dreams that well up from human hearts, when, lo, the world knows the birth of a rose.

Resting idly upon blue, hazy pillows of sky, with coverlets formed in white, fleecy clouds, breathing an incense distilled from the hearts of millions of soft-hued poppies, rests calm July, the Home of Repose.

Bearing aloft rank upon rank of stately blossoms that have fashioned their petals from the gold of the sunlight and woven into their hearts the love of their God, stands the month of glory that is the very breath of the sun— stately August, the Soul of Perfect Beauty.

September, the cosmic mother, whose innermost name is Purity and Peace, shines across the sky, building the treasures of her secret thoughts into rich boughs of waving goldenrod to caress the world, and to make it fairer while she holds it on her heart.

In the calm stillness, broken only by a fitful sighing through the trees, October, the Soul of Meditation, bends her head. Everywhere before and around her, magnificent forests are shedding half-wistful, golden tears for the summer's ebbing beauty, and half-fearful, crimson tears for the bleakness just ahead.

With majestic mien and stately tread comes royal November, crowned with garnered treasures and golden diadems, and bearing the queenly chrysanthemum. This cherished blossom of her heart was born out of a consciousness of over-pride. November breathes Temptation, and so subtly that even the brightest angels fell before it.

A song of achievement proclaims the coming of December, whose heart of hearts is Sacrifice. Her blossoms are wondrous tall and stately, with blood-crimson petals that enclose a golden heart. Involuntarily the Weavers of Flowerland give homage to them while the beauties of the other months lie half-forgotten. All during the long years the sacred blood-drop has lived in the heart of the little blossom whispering day by day the mystic meaning of its message until, filled with the joy of knowing, the flaming petals have grown and the golden heart expanded into the perfection of its stately beauty. For as the white petals shone with blood-crimson, this purest flower-soul awakened to the beauty of its cosmic mission, and knew that it must also take on the color of flesh and go out into the Flower world to bring its soul back into a realization of purity and love that manifests only in petals of purest white.

And so it is that each year when the Christ-life is born into the earth at Christmas time, the spirit of the Poinsettia comes in gorgeous sacrificial robes of red to bring its message to the world of flowers and of men.

A Message of Love

How the White Violet Grew

Close to the sod
There can be seen
A thought of God
In white and green.

It is so holy
And yet so lowly
Would you enjoy
Its grace and dower.

And not destroy
The living flower?
Then you must please
Fall on your knees.

—Anna B. deBary

There is a group of spirits to whom the angels are very tender during the interim between earth lives. This group is composed of beings who are endeavoring to come into the world but are prevented from doing so by the Law of Destiny because they have added lessons which they must first learn in the illumined regions of the heaven worlds. Into this group are gathered egos who are facing arduous lessons in another earth day and who must, therefore, come well prepared to meet the heavy trials and difficult situations that lie ahead. The angels know this and bestow much loving thought and tender care upon them during this time of preparation.

Between an expectant mother and the ego whose physical body is forming beneath her heart, there exists a magnetic band like a gleaming silver ribbon. This "ribbon" contains the story of their past relationship and the previous bonds that linked soul with soul and life with life. No such intimate relationship as mother and child ever marks the first earthly meeting between egos.

When the spirit approaches the confines of the physical world and is then forced to turn back, the readjustment to inner plane conditions is necessarily very difficult. Such a one is engaged in the payment of heavy debts due usually to deliberately and repeatedly thwarting other people's plans and resisting and defeating the realization of nobly conceived humanitarian endeavors.

There is always much pain and sorrow connected with an unsuccessful attempt to re-enter earth life again, and this suffering increases tremendously the bond between the ego and the prospective parents. Some times even the angels must veil their faces from the shadow which this sorrow casts as the silvery cord which unites mother and child is disconnected and floats away like an ethereal web of lace made heavy with the mist of tears.

Souls who have come so close to a physical environment are clearly conscious of the grief of their earthly parents and endeavor to assuage this sorrow as much as lies within their power. Accompanied by angels they many times float through the homes that have been prepared for them and leave a benediction of love and tender blessing as a gentle reminder of their presence. But since, unfortunately, it is not always possible for sorrow-stained eyes to discern their coming or for earth-dulled ears to hear their gentle whisperings, they have learned from their angel teachers to gather the gossamer wisps of the silver thread that bound mother to child, linking heart to heart, and which grew so heavy with tears when the bond was severed.

From this ethereal thread the angels have fashioned fragile flower petals of purest white and breathed upon their lips a delicate fragrance as sweet and deep as the love-bond between a mother and her unborn child. These delicate little flowers have been scattered all over the earth as a message of love from the spirit of the unborn to the mothers-to-be. This is how the White Violet has come to live in the world of men.

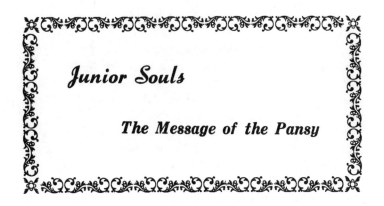

Junior Souls

The Message of the Pansy

A True Story for Children, and Grown-up Children, too.

Commemorative of the healing ministry of M. W.

And there is pansies—that's for thoughts.
—Shakespeare

This is the story of one of our younger brothers who knew an earthly life of only a few brief months, and yet in that time showed such love and self-sacrifice that children, and grown-up children, too, would do well to emulate it.

Pansy was a forlorn, grey kitten with a wistful flower-face, and big soft eyes which held memories of many sad experiences. For the eyes of animals tell of their numerous earth lives, even as do the eyes of human beings, and to know their story it is but necessary to understand how to read them.

One day while out trying to find what the big world contained, Pansy fell, and her frail little back was broken. Beneath the weight of pain her big eyes grew more wistful and the flower-face became thinner and more sharply defined.

About this time a blessed fairy godmother found Pansy and carried her away to live in a beautiful home by the sea. Then all the hard days were over, as the beautiful lady had a truly divine understanding of her younger brothers, and left nothing undone to fill Pansy's days with care and tenderness so that the little life might reap the full benefit of this earth-time experience. But despite all, the little body grew frailer and more attenuated. The tiny etheric double could be seen by sensitive eyes to be at times almost half free from the physical form, and it was only through her devoted response to the love and kindness lavished upon her that she was able to remain upon the earth plane at all.

Throughout the days while the fairy godmother was engaged in her ministrations of healing, Pansy would sit in the window and watch the Invisible Helpers — she thought they were angels—filling the godmother's room with beautiful thoughts and images. When the fairy godmother came home in the evening she gathered these for future use in helping to lift the sorrows of the world. While Pansy was unable to reason about these matters, she knew instinctively that these beautiful beings were bringing love and happiness to her fairy godmother, for when she came into the room her face would look as though the sun shone behind it. Then the little heart would beat very fast beneath its small, grey coat, and dancing lights would gleam within the tender eyes. But those who do not understand saw only a small grey kitten purring on the window ledge.

Outside the fairy godmother's window grew a beautiful white rose bush, and Pansy soon discovered that she used the roses for some special purpose in her work, since she tended them so carefully and always showed the deepest satisfaction and gratitude when finding a perfect blossom. At night Pansy was accustomed to watch the nature spirits building the flowers. In the lonely days before she had found the fairy godmother, she had passed all her nights so, and now that she discovered how much the rose bush meant to her guardian, she chose to make it her particular charge. On the nights of the full moon the nature spirits were especially active. At these times Pansy would sit carefully watching them all night long. Sometimes her little body grew very weary and the pain of the broken back was almost past endurance. But were not her nightly vigils a service and a sacrifice of love? It was in that spirit that Pansy, motionless and in silence, watched the nature spirits for hours as they fashioned the tender petals, and looked as with eyes transfixed upon the beautiful fairies as they breathed fragrance into the hearts of the blossoms. But of all this ethereal performance human eyes saw no more than a little grey kitten staring intently into the night.

For her loving attentions to the growing roses, Pansy felt herself richly rewarded when she saw her fairy godmother come in the morning to tenderly gather and carry away the fragrant white blossoms on their beautiful mission of healing. Whenever opportunity offered, Pansy would walk beside her beloved guardian so long as her small strength permitted, and when she could go no farther she still followed with sad eyes until the loved figure was completely lost to sight beyond the hills. Returning home alone, Pansy's little body grew so tired that she was forced to. rest many times in the shade of the tall grasses by the wayside, yet all the while the little heart beat happily and the wistful face was luminous with memories of tender caresses and gentle words.

Despite the great love that kept Pansy's faithful heart alive, the hold upon the delicate body grew less. One day the pain was almost unbearable, yet she crept to where the white roses grew to watch for the fairy godmother's coming. That day she was later than usual for many people had required her loving ministries. Often the crippled little grey figure would try to raise itself upon hearing a distant footfall, and the ebbing light would gleam anew in the shadowed eyes. But as the twilight fell on the sea, the tired little body fell forward on the grass, and when the fairy godmother arrived, the gentle heart had ceased to beat. Tenderly she lifted the slight form and carried it away, for in the greatness of her heart she finds room for all God's creatures. None are too small and humble to escape her love.

Reverently she placed Pansy's little body beneath the white roses where she had so often kept her long vigils. And now, for those "Who see, when the light of the Moon is full and the nature spirits are busiest, ofttimes amid the shadows comes a small grey form bounding as lightly as the fairies themselves, for the little back is no longer crooked or misshapen. And many times when the beautiful angels are filling the room with love thoughts for the fairy godmother, the little flower-face is close beside them. And they, too, smile tenderly upon it, for in their great hearts no love is ever too small to be unnoticed or go unrewarded. But for those who cannot see all this there is only a wee little mound beneath the grass upon which the white rose petals fall softly like flakes of perfumed snow.

The beautiful services which angels render to man do not embrace the whole of their mission to earth. Our younger brothers of the animal kingdom also come under their protective care. Those who are about the Father's business in the heaven worlds know that there is no real separation between the living and the dead, and so they return often to flood their former earthly dwelling places with love and blessings. In tenuous shadow forms, animals also revisit their former homes and stay close beside those whom they loved while in earth expression.

In that great aperture of light which divides the seen from the unseen and the visible from the invisible, and which to mortal knowing appears as a door or passage, stands a glorious being who directs and guides all those who pass back and forth between the inner worlds of the

Real and the outer realms of their reflection. This beautiful being is known as the Divine Mary, the Blessed Lady with Hands of Light—hands so illumined because of her constant and loving ministration for all living things. From her hands pour streams of effulgent light that flood eternally this Bridge of Transition between the living and the dead.

In flower-speech the angels make tangible this truth for all those who will receive it; and so they have fashioned the exquisite Pansy as a reflection of the multitudes of baby faces which hover ofttimes about the loved ones to whom they were loaned for so brief a stay. On their velvet petals are inscribed the loving, lisping baby prayers which encircle the earth when angels hang the curtains of twilight, star-pinned, from the skies.

And thus is it that this loved little blossom bears the name of Pansy—*pensez a moi*—think of me.

Acacia Blossoms

The light you bear yet do not see
Shall be a beacon to you and me,
Yet I shall be your guide.

—Woman's Message to Man

The long, soft stretch of sea lay shimmering in the waning light of late afternoon. Grey banks of clouds hung heavy above the horizon, shutting away that sense of the nearness of the infinite and that freedom of the soul which the spirit of the sea always gives. A man and a woman stood together upon the sand looking out over the dreary waste of waters as the ebbing tide moaned faintly against the shore like some heart in pain. The silence was broken by a sea gull calling softly to its mate. As the afternoon light fell lower, a long line of gold crept through the cloud bank and brought out in clear relief the outlines of a boat approaching the shore. As the boat drew nearer, the face of the Woman was illumined, while a shadow fell across the features of the Man. The Woman turned to the Man, and with a radiant smile stretched out her hands imploringly.

"Will you come with me?" she asked.

He turned away and looked steadfastly across the grey waters.

"Do you not see the golden light that is fast breaking through the leaden clouds? Oh, do come," she entreated, "for just beyond that curtain of gold which is every day growing more transparent, I can already see the Blue Hills of Attainment looming up against the sky with their shining crest of dreams. Their heights are so dazzling that I dare not as yet try to look at them; but if you will come with me, *together* we shall find their topmost peaks."

"I can see nothing," the Man declared, "but cloud banks hanging low above the sea. Why should we embark upon unknown waters in search of a strange adventure when there is so much to be done here? Why can you not stay with me and be satisfied with things as they are, be happy to live and love and work in the world we know?"

The Woman looked sadly away into the distance as she replied: "Really to understand and do our best work with the known, we must have some knowledge of the unknown. My work must reach back of effects that are seen and touch the causes that are unseen. Can you not realize that there is no barrier between us save the one which your own thinking has erected? We are both following the same path, only you have chosen the side that has been smoothed and leveled with much passing, while I am following the lonely way that but few have dared to venture upon as yet. Just so long as we go our separate ways the Work must remain incomplete and we shall stumble, maimed and crippled, through miserable failures and misunderstandings. The perfect fruition of our task can come only through a harmonious blending of our twofold power. For many thousands of years, through the strange [cacies] of life, we touched and parted only to find each new meeting half-shadowed with vague remembrances and troubled by half familiar dreams. How much longer will you delay the consummation of a plan that is divine in its completeness?"

"I do not understand," responded the Man; "I cannot see and I do not feel the strange call that lures you on. It seems to me that you are a prey to strange fancies, to bizarre notions that have no foundation in reality and truth. You are willing to forget love and duty for chimerical dreams.''

The Woman gazed at him compassionately as she listened, while a yearning tenderness that was half maternal swept over her. When he had ceased speaking she replied gently: ''If I had not first known this great love, I could never have found the key that unlocks the door of life's mysteries. No woman can begin to understand the divinity that sleeps in the heart of things until she has found her own divine self through the love of the soul.''

Her face grew rapt as she continued: ''Upon the way that leads to the crest of those blue Hills of Attainment, I can hear the heart beat of the centuries as the men and women of the human race climb together, and that indescribable light that crowns their summit is a reflection from the faces of those who have found the truth that abides there. There is an invisible, subtle cord that stretches between man and woman, binding them always together, unseen and even unsensed by many, but nevertheless the most powerful force in all the universe. When man comes into a realization of this law, he will know that he cannot hurt woman without hurting himself. Woman will know that she cannot rise without drawing man up.'' With these words she paused, and looking at him with the love of long ages welling up in her eyes, she continued: *''Neither can go all the way alone. There is a height that can only be attained when man and woman climb hand in hand together.''*

The boat had drawn close upon the sands and waited like some strange bird all poised for flight. The woman turned and regarded the man searchingly and earnestly. Again she spoke tenderly: ''Woman's soul leaps to the stars at one bound on wings of intuition, and there she

waits patiently while man climbs slowly and laboriously
by the long ladder of reason and intellect, but the two must
meet and reunite forever upon the summit of Divine Consummation. I shall be waiting for you always, oh soul of
my soul.'' Kissing him reverently on the brow, she turned
stumblingly toward the boat, blinded by tears.

Mute, silent, with a strange ache at his heart, the man
watched the boat slip away over the grey waters. As the
distance between them increased he felt sensibly the drawing of the cord that bound them together, and at the same
time a strange premonition thrilled through him that some
day he, too, must travel that same way. Almost unconsciously he strove to image the blue Dream Hills against
the horizon, and as he did so he saw the great mists part
above the boat and a golden star shining over it. At the
same time the invisible cord lengthened and lengthened,
but *he felt in his heart that it could never break.*

Every day the angels send their helpers out through
the earth world to gather up all the ideals and conceptions
that are born of humanity. They are ever on the watch for
beautiful dreams that are floating through the ethers; they
gather the essence of noble aspirations and the fragrance
of many deeds that are unsung and unheralded; these they
bear into the realms which the angels call home, and there
they are fashioned into flowers that the angels give back
again to the earth. Every flower is born of a beautiful
conception, or typifies some noble ideal that lives in the
hearts of humanity.

To symbolize the beautiful bond between man and
woman the angels gave birth to the Acacia. And that is
why it has been chosen by one of the foremost mystic
Brotherhoods, whose rites are founded upon the amal-
gamation of the masculine and feminine principles, for
ceremonial use as a symbol of Life Eternal and of Love
Immortal.

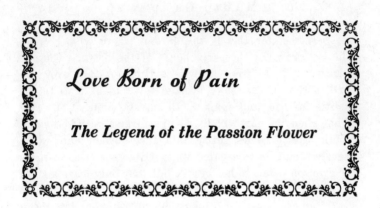

Love Born of Pain

The Legend of the Passion Flower

> Oh heart, oh blood that freezes
> Blood that burns,
> Earth's returns
> For whole centuries of folly,
> Noise and sin,
> Shut them in,
> With their triumphs and their glories and the rest—
> Love is best.
>
> —*Robert Browning*

The emotions belonging to the lower planes of the Realm known as Desire, give forth their life notes in a swirling mass of form and color, and here, too, the angels find work to do. Out of this maelstrom of smiles and tears, of hopes and disappointments, of fear and pain, in which the greater portion of humanity builds so unconsciously, yet nevertheless so constantly, the angel-helpers are busily engaged in weaving flower patterns that shall take form and grow upon the earth. Many flowers live and blossom as symbols of this influence generated by the thoughts and desires of men and women in the world.

There is a vast garden where gorgeous blossoms flame with lavish, crimson beauty. Even the sun seems to catch the reflection of their vivid light and shines here with a ruddier hue. All the air is still and heavy with a languorous perfume, for this is the garden where only Passion Flowers grow. In the early hours of the dawn, when the spiritual essence from heaven is being wafted over the earth and it is easiest to awaken the soul of man to the realities of life, and again in the mystic hour of the twilight, when the earth holds silent converse with the stars, a fair Spirit comes softly into this garden and walks eagerly along its variegated ways. Often she tries to press the crimson petals to her breast, but they only leave a stain of dark and sombre hue, and fill her heart with a strange yearning. She must for a long time turn disconsolate away —for the Spirit of Happiness can never find here a permanent place in which to abide.

The flowers of the garden grow more luxuriantly abundant and more wildly beautiful, while with each visit the Spirit of Happiness becomes frailer and more attenuated, until at last her gentle presence is like a shadow of some sweet half-remembered thing.

One day she comes into the garden very slowly, but still bending eagerly above the brilliant flowers, her fragile fingers scarcely having the strength to make their wonted scarlet impress on her breast. As she turns wearily away she falls unconscious to the ground, while a faint, sickening pollen sifts rapidly over her until she is almost lost to sight.

Suddenly a chilling wind sweeps over the garden and all the Passion Flowers droop limply on their stems, while a rare, white blossom that does not seem to belong to earth stands like a holy presence in their midst.

Under this new influence, the Spirit of Happiness revives and struggles to her feet. Eagerly she laves her bruised heart in the softness of its perfume, and her fingers lose their crimson stains amid the velvet of its petals.

The Passion Flowers droop lower and lower on their stems until their faces are completely hidden in the dust, while the strange white blossom grows taller and fairer and fills the garden with its heavenly glory.

"Happiness is too rare an attribute of the soul to be played with idly," say the angels, as leaning over the rim of the world they look into the prostrate garden below. "The flower of Love was not born a day too soon, for Happiness could no longer have survived amid such loneliness and pain."

A great wave of light suffuses the garden. One cannot tell whether it comes from the white flower that lifts its face so proudly to the stars, or from the faces of the angels as with folded wings and quiet hands they kneel to pray.

A Symphony of Lilies

*"God grows weary of great kingdoms but
never of little flowers."*

The breath of twilight fell softly on the garden, like some haunting, half-forgotten melody of fragrance. A symphony in white and gold, the garden lay all sweet and quiet beneath the opal-tinted sunset sky. Lilies, lilies—there were lilies everywhere. From rare exotics, steeped in their own rich perfume, to the tiny white blossoms with the kisses of the woodland on their lips.

To the Woman with the Heart of Tears, they brought a message of peace from their fragrant depths. In their pure, white beauty with golden hearts, she likened them to her own Lily-child, a little girl who had been wont to play there in the long ago. But that was when the Woman held the light of summer in her heart.

One night when the stars were shining and the Lilies bowed their heads beneath a grief of pearly dew-drops, the soul of the Lily-child was borne into God's keeping as softly as the sweetness of her garden was wafted upward on the wings of night. It was over the little heart that loved them so well the Lilies grew fairest and the blossoms were sweetest. When the Woman with the Heart of Tears rumpled them in her grief they shed a perfume that was like a benediction over her. Sometimes she even fancied that the soul of her Lily-child breathed again in their beauty and that the aroma of her love welled up from their perfect hearts.

One autumn evening, when the winds were playing little minor melodies with the wrinkled leaves, and the Lilies, like haunting memories, stood white, and tall, and still, the Woman with the Heart of Tears saw as she knelt among them, a sleeping child half-hidden in their perfumed shadows. A little waif perhaps, yet akin in her wondrous fairness to the Lily-child of the long ago. The golden hair was tangled amid the soft, white petals. The baby hands clutched a mass of wilted blossoms to her breast. She had wandered into this sanctuary guarded only by the sentinel Lilies. But they knew no difference, and clustered as lovingly about this pretty head as they nestled over the tender heart which for so long had lain cold and still.

In some strange way in which sadness was interwoven with a sort of minor sweetness, and tenderness was blended into pain, the little one smiled the essence of her dreams deep into the Woman's Heart of Tears. The breath of the drowsy Lilies stole over her in cadences of unwritten music while these words in lilting measures of fragrance, awoke into insistent melody in her heart: ''Whoso shall receive one such little child in My Name receiveth Me.''

The smiles that played across the little face were to the Woman with the Heart of Tears like the caresses of a sunbeam on delicately chiseled marble. The eyes that suddenly opened and looked into her own, were stars that had drifted down from the sky, still retaining some of the blue of their heavenly setting. With all a child's intuitiveness, she felt the yearning mother love bent above her. Reaching out her little hands with the careless, happy abandon of childhood, her baby laughter awakened an echo in the Woman's Heart of Tears which has been locked with sorrow since the little grave was made like a scar on the fair face of the garden. As she gathered the little child close into her lonely life, her tears fell softly on the crushed Lilies and brightened them as a new love awakened in her heart.

With the birth of this love came the light of a great understanding, the understanding that is inevitably found in the shadow of a love that is tinged with the divine. There beside the little bed where the sweet dreams of the Lily-child had taken tangible form in the Lily blossoms that bent above her, the Woman with the Heart of Tears learned that Love is the magic key of life and its infinite mysteries. The immutable law of compensation was invested with a power and a beauty she had never known before. She realized how infinitely good it is to know there is no cloud too dark for the sunlight to dissolve, no face so fair that it may not be stained with tears, and yet be fairer for them. It is only Love that purifies sin, makes sorrow a sacred thing and sets resignation like a star upon the brow of pain.

The incense of buried hopes came to her revivified in the glorious theme that angels sing before the Throne of God: "And now abideth faith, hope and love, these three, but the greatest of these is love."

In the vista of coming years, filled with possibilities stretching away before her, the tinge of pain which had shadowed all things, fell away. The world was golden-hued. She knew that love chords were striking deep into her heart the knowledge of the brotherhood of all mankind, breathing through her soul the ineffable harmony of her oneness with Infinity. This is the divine conception of Love.

—:—

When the night winds bowed the Lilies low upon their slender stems, the little mound beneath them was covered with the tender green of heartsease. And the fragrance of the garden seemed to melt into song—a symphony of Lilies.

77

The Cathedral of Night

An angel's wing beats at every window,
But only listeners hear and rise.

—Anon

The soft purple portals of the twilight having receded, there stands revealed the vast Cathedral of Night, dusty with longings, and shadowed with dreams, thick-set with points of gold flame that glitter and sparkle, and shower their secrets upon the heart of a sleeping world.

The interior of this imposing cathedral is the home of ineffable harmony and rhythm. The vast expanse is supported by infinite vistas of spiral columns formed in exquisite symmetry. Standing like the soul of some rare marble transformed into the Spirit of Youth, of Innocence, of Gladness, of Beauty, they give forth an ethereal effulgence of Light. Between these columns, fragrant aisles lead to an altar gleaming in its snowy whiteness like the purest alabaster. In wonderful perspectives these fairy-like colonnades stretch away into the distance, more beautiful as they recede until they lose themselves about the altar in a white and luminous ecstasy.

Suddenly the light is intensified. Notes of a triumphal chorus sound in the distance, coming nearer and nearer until all the vast cathedral is vibrant with music. Gradually every atom of space is filled—filled with the spirits of little children, joyous, radiant, free.

From their physical homes, while the little bodies are stilled in sleep, the souls waft away into the quiet Cathedral of Night. Here they form beautiful friendships with other souls of children who are also temporarily freed from their bodies of earth. Guided and directed by wise and loving angel-teachers, they are learning through joyful play to weave with golden threads into their earth lives some faint reflections from the heaven world. Beautiful angels gather these spirits into long, white processions that wend their countless ways through the Cathedral. First they enter the Hall of Silence, guarded by immense gates of gold that always swing wide, inviting whomsoever wills to enter, and never closing save at the sound of a spoken word, when, by some strange magic they become immense, impenetrable barriers, shutting out the exquisite beauties which lie just beyond them.

The walls of this Hall are composed of innumerable mosaics built of dreams. They form a symphony of iridescent, living, changing colors. Some of the patterns are oddly fanciful, others are captivatingly beautful, while others are so weird and strange that there are those who stand lost in wonderment before them. Each one who enters here finds a pattern to study. (For are we not all dreamers at heart?) Some of these dreams sparkle and glow with all the brilliancy of ever-increasing life because they have been brought to fruition upon the earth; others, half-shrouded in twilight shadows, are slowly vanishing into the dark things forgotten. They are unable to endure because they have never been given life in the world of men. (Souls there are who see with tender yearning that many of the fairest are thus drifting away.)

The floor of this Hall of Silence is of soft light and is like the mists of a spring day that rise all silver and cream from the heart of a river. The walls become fairer and more luminous the higher they ascend until they are lost in an indescribable splendor in infinite space. The patterns are constantly changing as new dreamers enter the Hall and there inscribe their dreams. One of the principal truths taught by the angel-teachers is the inestimable soul value to be gained by frequenting the Hall of Silence, and the significance it assumes in terms of knowledge, guidance and comfort in times to come for all mankind.

On leaving this Hall many of the children see a beautiful Spirit, distinguishable wherever she goes by the jewel worn upon her breast. This jewel grows larger and brighter with every service rendered to a needy one. When bestowing such help it sparkles with a glorious light. This is the Spirit of Service. Never is she found alone, but always among the throngs. Where the dark shadows fall longest and deepest, the light from the precious jewel upon her heart gleams like a star of love falling upon a weary world and soothing it into an infinite peace.

Sun-bright rays from the Spirit of Love shine upon and transfigure those whose hearts and hands are learning to follow in her ways of helpful ministry. As the souls go forward in companies they find the entrance to a vast room, a room whose dimensions beggar description. Across its ever-open portals the rays of a brilliant Star casts its light, and everyone who comes within its radius must enter in. The interior of this room is formed of numerous sheaths of pearls. The floors that stretch away into infinite distance and the walls whose boundaries are beyond vision are all aglimmer with their soft sheen. The light here is quiet and subdued like the light of a young moon shining in deep forests. Stealing through the air are dreamy minor melodies played on harps of gold.

Some of those whom the Star has guided to the door come with wailings and sore cries of pain; others come willingly with signs of gratitude for what they recognize as an opportunity to learn important and much needed lessons. After its earthly sojourn each and every soul must again cross this same threshold, for it is here that the Law of Cause and Effect impresses its record in pictured form. Mortals have come to know this place as the Hall of Sorrow. Its most precious gems are formed of the crystallized tears of humanity. Many beautiful pearls of sacrifice and of renunciation are to be found here. These are shown to the ones who have the eyes to see by the angels who serve as teachers. Every day additional pearls are placed in the beautiful structure; none are ever lost. This is why the room must be so large and why its boundaries are immeasurable.

The most beautiful thing in this spacious chamber of light is the Pearl Altar. Each gem is perfect in size, color and shape and is illumined with a tender, yearning beauty. These are the crystallized tears of mothers. It is at this altar that spirits in sorrow come nearest to God. It is here that the very Spirit of Sorrow lives when away from her home in the heaven world. In this high realm she is always found near the Spirit of Love. So it is that sorrow ever broods near the white glory of Love. Such is the teaching of the angels to the souls of visiting children, and this knowledge is deeply engraven upon their hearts so that the earth experiences to which they return may become more understandable. After such instruction many recognize intuitively the Spirit of Sorrow as sweet and fair and friendly, and so losing all fear of her, greet her with outstretched arms. The Spirit of Sorrow is always robed in white, symbolizing the fact that she entertains no regrets. When a soul has recognized its true mission, sorrow disappears because it has become transmuted into love. The egos of the children are enjoined to remember that to an awakened spirit sorrow is but the crucible in which to test the strength of character.

Besides the entrance to this vast Hall of Sorrows stands a figure who seems the essence of light itself. Surrounded by a halo of quivering radiance that extends far beyond the line of vision and piercing deep to the heart of everything it touches, it draws forth an echo in reflected splendors. Many souls come from the Hall of Sorrow, some in companies, others alone, but on each and all this brilliant Spirit casts a ray of light. Few among them are conscious of the light that encircles them, and only rare and exceptional souls are able to see the sublime Spirit.

Very rarely is this Spirit visible to those who come forth in companies; when seen it is almost invariably by one who walks alone. The angels explain that this is the sublime Spirit of Truth. In her real home, in the heaven world, she lives closer to God than does any other Spirit save that of Love. Though egos may stand in the light that emanates from her, they may never come close to the great Spirit. When one attempts to reach her, she always recedes; but the LIGHT BECOMES GREATER. No one is ever conscious of the full glory of this great light, excepting those who bear in their hearts an impress from the Hall of Sorrow.

In vast companies the souls of the children gather around the glorious White Altar of the Cathedral. This is the altar of Love and it is illumined with the pure, white light that descends from the very throne of God. The light that emanates from this altar floods the majestic edifice throughout its length and breadth and depth. The angels tell the children how light always portrays love. Never can there be light without love, since the latter is the cause of the former. Whenever they see the light of a new day they must remember that it is an expression of God's love for the world. Whenever they see the sun, the heart of our planetary system, they must know that it, too, is a symbol of God's love.

Hovering above this altar is a congregation of souls awaiting the summons to birth again. Each one, as the Angel of Life calls, gathers an offering from the altar of Love to carry away in its heart to the world, for these are God's sweetest messengers to man. Beyond the altar of

Love is the entrance into what appears to be the domain of Shadowland. As the children approach this entrance, they hesitate as though a wave of pain sweeps over them; a shadowy gloom permeates the space which is outlined with a soft frieze of tears. Countless little ones enveloped in the soft shades are faintly discernible, and a plaintive wailing as of regrets sounds from orchestras formed of shadows.

The angels explain that this is the home of those who are waiting to take up their earth lives again, and that when the Angel of Life calls them, they must go, each one into homes that are foreign and strange, and where they will not be welcomed. This is why they intuitively shrink from going forth and why they are enveloped in shadows. They do not live as close to the great altar of Love as do those who are going into love-homes where their arrival is awaited with fond and eager expectancy. These little ones of the Shadowland sometimes forget to take an offering from the Love altar when they go forth into the earth world, and because of this lack in their hearts, their lives will be very hard until they find love in serving others. As we sow, so we must reap; these unfortunate ones have sown in the darkness; now they must reap shadows until sorrow and suffering shall have brought them into a realization of the perfect Law.

Suddenly across the air steal ineffable harmonies which rise from a symphonic play of colors. Soft lavenders melt into exquisite greys, and violet hues interlace with rose in changing tones of beauty so rare and delicate that they seem but drifting gossamer dreams. Each color breathes in fragrant music, soft, elusive—stealing close in half-plaintive strains, only to lose itself in the distance with fairy-like echoes. Floating, shifting, weaving and parting, they open alluring vistas of a dream-world beyond. Mountains and meadows, flower-covered valleys and plains stretch away in a strange, unearthly beauty illuminated and irradiated by a golden sun. The light has penetrated to the heart of every tree and flower and left therein a ray of itself to testify to the glory of light and love. The air is so luminous with these coruscating colors that no mortal eye could bear the brilliancy for long.

From the heart of this dreamland comes a feminine figure of superhuman majesty, and yet not so fair as the angels. She is attended by many beautiful figures who are scattering dream-scented poppies along her way. Sweet immortelles and the perfume of heartsease are mingled with the fragrance of her thoughts in tender greeting. "Who do you think I am?" she asks. The children are silent in an awed ecstasy. "I am the Spirit of Death," comes her reply.

To the wondering exclamations which greet this announcement she volunteers further information about herself. "Yes, I know," says she, "that poor deluded mankind has always pictured me as a creature carrying a skull and cross bones, or in other terrifying forms that instill in mortals a general fear of my presence; but if they only understood, they would know me as a friend. The more man learns of me the more shall he know of himself."

Gently caressing the groups that have gathered near her, she continues: "I love all who come to me, and I take each one to my heart as a mother does a tired child. They are nearly all just children after all—some of them very tired and most of them sorely frightened at the change. Teach the world, my little ones, when you return, that there is nothing to fear. Death is but a passing from a dream into reality—the reality that lies back of the dream. All these who attend me receive and care for the little ones who come from earth and have none of their loved ones here to meet them and assist them in accommodating themselves to their new environment. The service I most gladly render," she adds softly, "is the stilling of a tired heart and giving rest to a weary soul."

85

The curtain of colors rises again, revealing scenes of entrancing beauty and breathing music so strangely sweet that even the angels are constrained to pause and listen. The Spirit of Death tells the children that in this world of color every movement emits a sound. The air is so rarefied and the vibrations so fine that souls there can hear the sound of things growing; the trees, flowers and grasses unite in a song of wonderful harmony. Added to this is the symphony composed of the tones emitted by the thoughts and movements of the angels and those in their charge. Concerning this music of the subtler realms, the Death Angel tells her eager listeners: "The nature spirits also give such music to the world, but those who live upon earth are so immersed in sounds of materiality that they cannot hear this heavenly music. By reason of their sensitiveness, the birds come close enough to the music of the heaven world to suggest at least echoes from these celestial harmonies.

"From the color tones of the higher planes the flowers have caught their variegated hues, and the love thoughts of the angels are transmitted in their fragrance. Your thoughts of love, beauty and truth take on the form of flowers in this sphere. These the angels mould into earthly blossoms, and give them back to enrich your life. The angels, moreover, impress their own love-thoughts into these same flowers which become as it were, an emanation of their very being. So when next you inhale a flower's fragrance, remember you are receiving a message of love from the angel who made it. What has been said of beautiful thoughts holds true also of ignoble thoughts. They, too, become externalized. They become the frosts and droughts that wither and blight the blossoms of goodness and truth. But before long the Spirit of Love will so permeate the physical world that all unkind and untrue thoughts will be dissolved. Then the earth will become attuned to the higher octaves, and its inhabitants will see and understand

86

many things that they do not now know. And most wonderful of all, nobody will be afraid of death. All will realize its true mission. Help me to bring that day nearer.''

Her smile was like the white fragrance of moonlight as once more the colors parted. When they closed again, the beautiful spirit had disappeared, leaving no sound save the music of her going.

But time hastens on and other lessons are yet to be given the children before the coming Dawn calls them away to take up their earth lives again. So guided by their angel-teachers, they press on toward a garden where large numbers are being instructed in painting the gorgeous color-tones of the sunset. As the throngs go forward, they pass a beautiful Spirit standing half in shadow, half in the light. In their haste, only a few heed her presence. At long intervals some one turns aside from the passing concourse long enough to touch the hem of her garment. When this happens a profound joy gives light to her countenance, otherwise saddened by the many who pass her unnoticed. This is the Spirit of Memory, whose place must long remain in the shadows. Rare is the soul who touches her garments, and thereby carries a recollection of the heaven world over into the consciousness of earth life. For every one that makes this contact there is a rejoicing in the heart of the Spirit of Memory, for such awakened souls become teachers upon earth of the truths of life everlasting.

One who has come to the Spirit of Memory is endowed with a vision that sees the light beyond the shadows even as we see the rainbow shining among the storm clouds. Such a one gladly shares the sorrows of humanity in a forgetfulness of self· Willingly he walks in the shadowy places that others struggling therein may have more of the sunlight. Gratefully does he choose the rough ways, for he knows that it is by following the road of pain that the soul may be most quickly conditioned to stand before the Shrine of the Spirit.

Soon the Egos we know as children find themselves in the midst of a fairy-like garden that looks as though it might be made of the rainbow. Twelve beautiful Spirits are grouped in a semi-circle near the entrance. The angel-teachers explain that these are the Spirits of the Hours. "There are twelve for the hours of the day and twelve for the hours of the night. They surround the earth, and their circle is never broken. The twelve Spirits who guard the night are now in the world wherein they form the other semi-arc of the circle.

"These Angels of the Night are busy gathering together the beautiful thoughts and the good deeds that have made their impress upon the earth during the day. These they bring back to the angels, whom you see at work here and who transform them into colors with which they paint the sky. Under the guidance of the Spirit of the Dawn and the Spirit of the Sunset, hosts of angel-helpers are teaching disembodied entities to work with the colors of the earth. While they appear transparent, they are in reality much more intense, and sparkle and glow with the radiance of life itself. Here are the brilliant reds of human life graduating into the higher octave of the rose-tones; the orange forces that magnetize physical existence and sound the call for service to humanity; tender greens that soothe in sweet compassion; blues of harmony and happiness melting into the soft azure of mystic dreams, and lavenders that breathe of sorrows divinely borne ascending into the violet lights of the spirit.

"This whole range of color is overshadowed by the glorious tints of love. Each day there must be some gold in the sunset because there have been love thoughts in the world, and this is their golden reflection. Far in the interior of the garden are other beings who are working with colors which no words can describe. These will not be available for use on earth until the children who are drawn here night after night have grown up and learned how to apply them in their earth lives. The earth will then be sufficiently rarefied to contact these finer colors."

Near the entrance of the garden a fountain is spraying perfumed waters of many-colored hues. Upon the myriads of fragrant flowers dreaming in its soothing mist are some that resemble the mystic lotus blossoms of the East. The spirits we know as children learn that this is the Fountain of Hope. Its waters are never stilled, since "hope springs eternal." The robes of the Spirit of Hope are formed of all the vari-colored hopes that live in the world, and the mystic flowers on her brow come from the heart of the waters.

While the children are revelling in the entrancing beauties of the garden, they see a number of the inmates from the Shadowland approaching the fountain. In reply to their inquiries, the angels tell them that each one before going into earth life visits the Fountain of Hope. As we have already learned, souls from the Shadowland sometimes fail to take an offering from the Altar of Love, but they never leave without partaking of the ever-renewing Waters of Hope.

The circle of the Hours is now changing in a rhythm of stately measures. The Spirits of the Night are seen in the distance, and the angels of the Morning Hours are coming close to the edge of the world as Dawn appears on the horizon in a multi-colored glory. The predominating tone of her coming sounds the golden note of Love, for Love it is that is calling the egos who are still bound by earth bodies, and who, in response to the call, slip gently and silently away.

Wise mothers move softly when precious souls come back to them in the arms of the morning. They bend low and see the light of heaven that still lingers in their eyes. They kneel in adoration before the angelic fragrance of their lips.

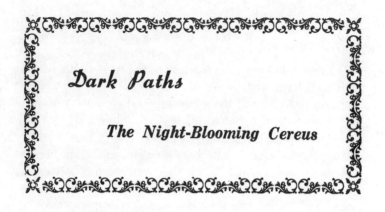

Dark Paths

The Night-Blooming Cereus

Wondrous truths and manifold as wondrous,
God hath written in those stars above,
But not less in the bright flowers under us
Stands the revelation of His love.

—Longfellow

Angels are divided into groups according to talent
and ability in the same way as are human beings. Also as
with us, these various groups each have a distinguishing
badge or insignia. There is, however, a very important difference between the human and the angelic symbols of
identification. Among the angels the signification of group
allegiance is one of attainment and not a mere decorative
motif to be attached to the outer person. It is entirely a
quality of soul, a development of the spirit, and can, therefore, be seen only by those who have eyes to see.

There is one group who perform a particularly colorful and beautiful service for man in recognition of which
its members wear upon their foreheads a star-like glittering jewel of light. They are the group who see the sorrow
caused by death upon the earth, and who devote themselves
to its alleviation. Their service goes on uninterruptedly,
and in its performance they are of all angels the most
blessed. The Death Angel is always followed by a glittering
train of these ministering angels who sing of the glories of

life immortal. They fill the silent chamber of death with a flood of light and power that comes like soft heavenly balm to the hearts of the sorrowing—an emanation of that great peace which passeth all understanding.

Many persons there are who will testify that in their insupportable moments of grief-stricken separation caused by the loss of a best beloved, they have been conscious of the presence of these angelic messengers. Surely among the many and varied offices of love and service performed by these angelic brothers of man this is one of the most beautiful and far-reaching in its effects. Not only do they ease the agony of the parting, but they place within the sorrowing heart a tiny flower of hope to be nurtured in love until it grows, expands, and blossoms into a certainty of consciousness that *there is no death.*

Since this is the most glorious realization that man can know in his present earth day, the flower-conception embodying it is of corresponding splendor. That flower is the Night-blooming Cereus.

"This transition is but a death that is no death." So sing the angelic voices to all responsive hearts, and all the while the bright star flower of hope takes root, and at length brings forth new blossoms. But this is not all; there still remains much work to be done before the veil of despair, doubt and uncertainty which darkens the vision of the masses is lifted. And so long as this remains true, the gorgeous Cereus blooms only at night, and despite the beauty and magnitude of its blossoms, it lives but a few short hours in the oppressive and uncongenial atmosphere of earth.

It is only when the long shadows of evening fall, and the earth is stilled in the calm benediction of the approaching night, that the white petals of the Cereus begin to unfurl. When the mystic midnight hour approaches, its sweet golden heart is laid bare to the stars. One of the most fragrant of all flowers, being heavy with the prayers of angels, it stands a white sentinel of light proclaiming the glory tidings of the new day just breaking above the world wherein "death shall be swallowed up in victory" and "God shall wipe away all tears."

When man's realization of this truth shall have become clear and strong, and he shall have learned to walk in the Light even as He is in the Light, the beautiful Cereus, symbol of such recognition of life immortal, will possess renewed strength which will enable it to unfold its soft petals even before the noonday sun. As yet it must needs fold its wings over the sweetness of its heart and await the day when man will live in the consciousness of his eternal nature, following which its ethereal and fleeting glory will become immortal upon the earth.

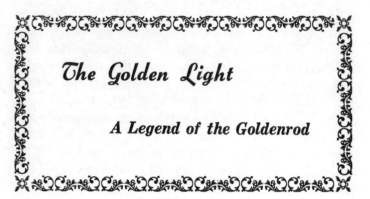

The Golden Light

A Legend of the Goldenrod

GOLDENROD

When the wayside tangles blaze
In the low September sun,
When the flowers of summer rays
Drop and wither one by one,
Reaching up through brush and brier
Sumptuous brow of heart and fire
Flaunting high its wind rocked plume,
Brave with wealth of native bloom—
Goldenrod!

Nature lies disheveled, pale,
With her feverish lips apart—
Day by day the pulses fail
Nearer to her bounding heart.
Yet that slackened grasp doth hold,
Store of pure and genuine gold
Quick thou comest strong and free
Type of all the wealth to be,
Goldenrod!
—Elaine Goodale Eastman

As man is learning to understand and commemorate
the mystery of the changing seasons, so also the angels
know and keep sacred vigil at these holy times. We must

95

ever remember, however, that the angelic life wave touches a much higher plane of spiritual consciousness than that of the human. Consequently, the angels know a deeper meaning and receive a greater inflow of spiritual ecstasy at the time of the four seasonal solar festivals.

As man worked in ages past with the animal kingdom and helped in the formation of animal bodies, so are the angels giving their ministrations to the kingdom of plants.

One of their most joyous tasks has been to embody within the Flower Kingdom the highest ideals and noblest conceptions of man. Joyously they have woven all the fragrance and beauty of his highest thoughts and deeds into flower-symbols of tender loveliness.

How gladsome is their rejoicing when they discover one who, though still wearing a garment of flesh, is able to see and understand their work with the flowers and to interpret the mystic messages which are inscribed upon each colorful petal.

There is a time of the year which the scientists term the autumn equinox and which the mystic knows as the season of the great spiritual inflow. The angels, too, reverently observe this sacred festival, for they are privileged to see from their high place in the etheric realms that Cosmic Ray of Light which gradually descends upon the earth, enveloping and suffusing the planet until, to eyes not blinded with the veil of mortality, it appears to become a body of radiant, vibrant gold.

This Light grows brighter and more powerful until it penetrates into the very heart of the earth. It is then that the angels can no longer contain their great joy for the work of redemption which they know is being accomplished both for man and the planet upon which he dwells. And so they fill all the world with their songs of rejoicing.

Sometimes there are those who are pure enough to glimpse this great Light and to catch an echo of this angelic chorus, and so have called this time of spiritual ecstasy the Holy Night.

The angels labored long and reverently in the work of transmitting a bit of the essence of this Divine Light into its spiritual prototype, the flowers. At last their work was complete, and in soft, feathery plumes of golden radiance there blooms each year in the autumn-time the flower that symbolizes the down-pouring of the Great Impulse. Gleaming in yellow tones of the Christ's own color, the Golden Rod breathes forth a reflection of the rays from the Sun.

An ancient Gaelic legend gives to September the synonym of peace because this was the birth month of the Immaculate Mother of Him whose name is Peace. To commemorate this truth in flowers the angels have given to the earth a preponderance of golden blossoms in the autumn time.

A poet who has caught this message sings:

> *Oh, Peace! the fairest child of heaven*
> *To whom the sylvan reign was given.*

During the months in which the golden Light of the Cosmic Christ is suffusing the earth, the angels have wreathed it in blossoms of the same lovely hue. Chief among these is the Golden Rod which carries the message of the new ingress of Life and Light, when "peace is on the earth and in the air."

These brilliant blossoms, woven by angels to bear the love messages of Christ for man, were aptly chosen as the national flower by the great pioneering people of the new world whose ideal is Peace and whose dream is Fellowship. And so it is that during the sacred months of the Ingress, this lovely symbol of Its coming gives forth the glad tidings in showers of blossoms, and heralds in its beauty that angelic chorus soon to be sounding: "Peace on earth and good will among men."

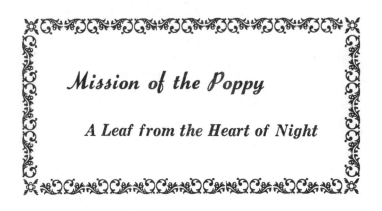

Mission of the Poppy

A Leaf from the Heart of Night

The sleep flower sways in the wheat its head,
Heavy with dreams as that with bread.

—Anon

The long line of regular, white buildings lie tense with silence beneath the quiet hands of night. In their soft, mystic beauty, quivering stars illumine the darkness. The world lies sleeping amid the hovering silences. Within the wide halls are grotesque shadow-forms and soft, shaded lights that wax and wane.

The flaming silence is interrupted by rasping tones of call-bells, or the soft monotone of sleep broken by sobbing, intermittent breathings of pain and the hurrying footfalls of white-clad nurses on their gentle missions.

Upon a slender cot a figure swathed in bandages tosses restlessly, shivering and moaning as though fighting some intangible enemies unseen by mortal eyes. The shaded lights flare and flicker with the uneven breath of the night wind, showing in faint outlines the queer figures bending above the prostrate body.

Through the softened light, tenuous forms dance in demoniacal joy. Towering above the bed and urging the strange beings on to greater efforts is a hideous specter fearful to behold. The ill-formed figure seems half a part of the fantastic shadows that reel about the dimly-lighted room. From the swaying arms projects a wand with a dully gleaming red point. When this weird being concentrates his gaze upon this point the room is filled instantly with sinister forces in an atmosphere of murky red. Snatching up waves of these thick colors, dozens of tiny fiends bind them about their victim's hands and feet, causing him to writhe in paroxysms of agony, much to their sadistic delight.

Suddenly a beneficent figure appears on the scene and well-nigh paralyzes the fiends. A rose-hued light fills the room. The Spirit of Healing now, as always, has come to battle for the body of man. Enveloped in an aura of loving service the Spirit muses: "Oh, body of man, how little you have understood me. How much closer I may come to nature than to you! The earth yields to me her secrets. Mine is the tender soothing that lures you into the forests. I live in the fragrant breath that greets you from the hills· The flowers know me and the animals seek me. But you alone, oh man, whom mind has set upon the path midway between the flowers and the gods, repulse me. Only when the ends of pain have made thee prostrate may I prove my power. Come forth, messengers of sleep, my most faithful servitors."

Here the opalescent, rose-hued light deepens, and innumerable little fairies trip across the pillows, scattering fragrant petals of sleep over the now quieting body. Gradually the muscles grow less tense, and the distorted features relax. In vain the fiends throw out their baleful thoughts of murky red. They are instantly caught and transformed into soft, shaded rose-tones of love and healing as the night wears on apace.

But mortal eyes can see only white-clad nurses busy with their gentle ministrations.

Among the dusky shadows of a far-off room the Heal-Spirit stands disconsolate. In vain the soothing messengers scatter perfumed petals of sleep across the bed. Their tender, roseate glow turns into lingering tones of ashen grey, and soon they shiver and crumple with an ebbing sweetness.

Even the fiends seem to have grown weary of watching their victim's suffering as the veins swelled and flamed beneath their cruel, crimson bars.

No sounds to mortal ears intrude upon the silence save the breathing of the nurse as she bends over her patient with soothing hands.

Suddenly a rush of light hovers above the bed, and from out its radiance sounds a voice; "Cease your parleying above this last remnant of my mortality. I am the ego who fashioned these atoms into the form they now hold; mine is the power to disintegrate them. Through aeons of time and ceaseless strivings, I have found the way that leads to infinite peace. By the light of Cosmic knowing I have learned how poor a thing is this frail tenement in which I live. Oh, house of mine, together we have wrought and suffered, and from the heart of you my soul shall build a nobler temple in which to dwell. Upon these atoms, before I resolve them back into that order which is chaos, I shall leave the impress of divinity."

As the voice comes to silence, a quivering light runs through the body. For a moment it rests about the head and forms an aureole of glory as the silver cord is severed and an eager soul set free.

Mortal mind knows only that the labored breath has ceased and that Death with solemn majesty has come to claim her own.

The long line of regular, white buildings lies expectant with awakening beneath the early morning sky. The stars disappear within the voluminous white folds of her garments. The world is stirring to the miracle of day. The first rays of the rising sun fall through an open window and lighten waiting corners out of their accustomed gloom. Within the room a soft silence reigns. Only a few frail petals, like shriveled rose leaves, droop heavily above the bed in evidence of the combat that had only just been waged there with such fierceness.

But mortal eyes see only a white clad figure bending tenderly above the quiet form.

The angels wished to give to man, through the medium of the Flower world, a symbol of the infinite intricacies of night when the body is laid aside to rest and to restore its powers while the indwelling spirit takes freedom to wing to far horizons. "White nights," says Walter Pater, "should not be nights of black forgetfulness but passed in continuous dreaming only half-veiled by sleep."

These white nights in remembrance! How blessed is their privilege. They know the call of the sinking ship, the pain of the hospital wards, the cry of the entombed miner, the voice of the battlefield, the frenzied inmates of a burning building, the misgivings or the calm of those making the transition of death.

Few there are as yet who keep these hours in holy remembrance and so the flower builded about this ideal is as fragile and tenuous as is this flitting memory. Its petals flutter and fall with the slightest swaying of the winds. Man's prolonged remembrance of the nights' activities will give increased strength and endurance to the Poppy that meanwhile sways in all its fragile beauty, indicative of the winged activities of the human soul when apart and free from its physical casement of the day.

If earth-dulled ears are not too heavy, one may listen and hear above these fields of lilting, swaying blossoms the fairy music of the Poppy song; "Partake of my sleep and remember."

Vale of Tears

How the Weeping Willow Came to Be

By the little river
Still and deep and brown,
Grow the graceful willows
Gently dipping down.

Were they water maidens
In the long ago
That they lean so sadly
Looking down below?

In the misty twilight
You can see their hair,
Weeping water maidens
That were once so fair.
　　　　—Walter Prichard Eaton

The long, graceful festoons of the Willow Tree have always been expressive of mourning. In one of David's most beautiful Psalms which describes the sorrow of the exiled Israelites, we learn of lamentations sounded to the music of harps, and that the instruments so used were later hung upon the Willow. The tree has thus become an emblem of sorrow and hence it is often said of one who is sad, that "He has hung his harp upon a willow tree."

103

The Willow has ever been associated with the sorrow that comes through death. In the earliest sacrificial ceremonials the victims were garlanded with its branches, and in this modern day it is one of the favored decorations of that sacred ground in which the bodies of the beloved dead are laid to rest. There is a special reason for this which was known and understood by man before the veil that separates the land of the living from that of the dead had become so dense as it is now.

Among those who must remain upon the earth, many have learned how wise and well it is to pray for the loved ones who have passed to the other side, but only a few as yet know that one of the first duties enjoined upon those who make the passage, is to pray for the sorrowing ones whom they have left in this outer plane of consciousness. And so it is that prayers of love, strength, healing and courage are continuously wafted back and forth between heaven and earth. Every day knows the agony of parting and the pain which can only be lessened through such an interchange of loving prayers between those on earth and those on the unseen side of life.

These love-prayers ascend and descend in streams of living force or light that play upon the earth in a perpetual radiance, for thought is creative and its interchange between newly-severed hearts is a source of power which the angels mass and use in their efforts to thin the veil now hovering between the seen and the unseen. With each passing year increasing multitudes are bearing joyful witness to the efficacy of this work.

That the still blinded earth children may have an increasing realization of this continuous communion between the ''here'' and ''there,'' they have moulded the essence of these healing prayers into the shadow-form of this beautiful tree. The strength of the prayers sent upward from the earth are builded into its roots and trunk. The loving messages of the souls newly released from the limitations of physical bondage, droop in a tender, pendant benediction woven into its branches to fall upon hearts that are still lonely and faces that are yet stained with tears.

Green is the color-tone of sympathy and compassion, and it is in the softest, most tender greens that the angels wrap this tree, a symbol of tears. Daily they whisper, as they bend above it: "There is no death for those who love, for love is life and life is love."

The Willow Tree must bear its synonym of tears until the sons and daughters of earth come to understand this message which the angels have imprinted within its heart, for it is only then that the separation in death can be no more.

Lost Ideals

The Song of a City Pavement to a Broken Flower

I have worn this day as a fretting, ill-made garment
Impatient to be rid of it,
And lo, as I drew it off my shoulders,
This jewel caught in my hair.

—*Anon*

Each year increasing numbers are coming into a realization of the nearness of the angelic hosts unto the world of men, but few as yet are aware of the far-reaching import of their services. This earth would have been dissolved in chaos long since were it not for their loving ministrations.

Wondrous is the vision of the shining hosts above our sleeping cities during the hours of the night. Evil thoughts and words and deeds of men hover above like great black birds of prey, ready to descend again as sickness, want, woe and various other ills that the spirit of man should never know.

Nightly come hosts of angel-servers to dissipate these miasmic forces in the glory of their transforming love. Busily during the silent hours they rain showers of golden blessings upon the sleeping earth, and when the multicolored bars of opalescent dawn play across the sky they wing their way, encircled by a medley of color and song athwart the far horizon and are lost to human view in the splendors of etheric mists. Their bright, loving eyes scan the world for sight of human sufferers who are forlorn or deserted, and whom they are ever ready to heal and bless.

One night during the silent watches, a bright being descended with all the glory of a falling star and bent above a bruised and broken flower lying forgotten upon a deserted city street. "A broken flower means lost ideals," murmured the angel. "Somewhere tonight a heart is heavy with sadness."

The angel bent above the little flower, and as he did so he was conscious of music sounding, music that rose in waves of strange tonal beauty from the depths below. Then he knew that he was listening to an echo of the experiences of the day just closed, as these still lingered in the impress they had made upon the city streets.

The thronging pavements of a metropolis are the white keyboards of humanity upon which the varied footfalls play. Stretching ever calm and quiescent they absorb and hold this human music. Oh, the quivering heartache that trembles through some note! He who listens well may hear the music of tear drops falling—falling. In glad arpeggios come the steps of youth, as light as the morning radiance and as fragrant with hope as the woodland flowers before the noonday sun has stolen the dew from their hearts.

Faltering minor notes of despair sometimes creep into the harmonies, so long drawn out that the very pavements are touched with sympathy. The hurrying rush of breathless crowds would wait and listen could they but hear even their faintest whisper. But alas, so intent are they upon mere outer knowing that heedlessly they pass, and only the pavements—the long white keyboards of humanity— register the song of sorrow.

In delicate trills that tremble with human sweetness, softly as cathedral music sounds the footsteps of the mother-soon-to-be. In the beauty of her passing shines the mystery of some enchanted dream.

Forming a deep undertone to the music, ring the footfalls of the lonely. So many are the notes sounding from here that it seems at times as though the other tones must all be crowded out. Yet beautiful they are to the listening ear—those lonely foot-tones. Some of them blend into rare combinations, giving forth such music as the world would never otherwise have known.

In all this pulsing, echoing orchestra there ever sounds an insistent note running through the lights and shadows, singing in octaves of majors and preludes of minors—the Mighty Chord of Unsatisfied Aspirations. Oh, the yearning music of this seeking multitude, aimlessly drifting or anxiously searching! A legato of unconscious pleading mourns, why? why? why? followed by a vast crescendo of sob-tones asking where? where? where?

As the shadows lengthen, there comes the weary toneless music made by tired feet. Have you ever listened to it, and wondered why in all God's world there should be a dissonant note in the hour that tolls the passing of the day when all the earth is encircled with prayer?

Did you ever listen for the gentle sighing that murmurs in the heart of night at the ceaseless rush of dancing music from the steps of those who, heedless of her matchless beauty, seek only the flickering will-o-the-wisps of pleasure?

But for those who understand—oh, the tender compensation of the night! The low, leaning night with its vast heart-beat of stars And the requiem of darkness that soothes the wounds and the heartaches gathered in the rush of day!

Listen to the music of the pavements with its thousand footnotes. Hear the faltering, hopeful, weary, radiant, dreaming, longing notes which all together form a chorus that blends into a divine unity of strange beauty, a stupendous shadow-song of the city.

As the angel lifted the little flower and laid it gently against his heart, he sighed softly, saying, "And he who lifts his soul above the clinging hands of earth may listen to her singing."

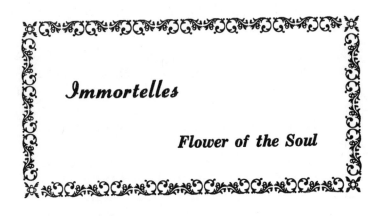

Immortelles

Flower of the Soul

The high that proved too high,
The heroic for earth too hard,
The passion that left the ground
To loose itself in the sky,
Are music sent up to God by
The lover and the bard.
Enough that He heard it once
We shall hear it by and by.
—Robert Browning

The air was very still in the Garden of the Soul; and a quiet calm pervaded the place. The broad Walk of Meditation that reached up toward the Gates of Knowledge was hedged on either side with the soft Jasmine of Memory. The Path of Retrospection, bordered with herbs that were bitter-sweet, grew dim in the silences of vague distances that led up to the very Shrine of Prayer. Here the air was cool and comforting, and filled with fragrance from the white lilies that were massed around the Shrine and which lifted their pure faces to the stars, freighted with the incense that rises from holy aspiration.

Before this shrine, the Woman with the Tired Heart liked best to linger. Here she struggled to find within her tortured soul something of the gentle peace that enveloped the shrine of Prayer. Each day when her strength permitted, she would begin anew the pilgrimage that led to the far slopes of the garden which were always bare and cold.

"It was here that I buried my dream of happiness," she whispered through her tears.

This end of the garden was always strangely barren. In vain the Woman with the Tired Heart had planted balm and heartsease over it. She had watered the growing plants with her tears, yet they drooped and withered, leaving the place bare and lifeless. It was like some wound in the heart that can never be healed.

"Such a tender dream it was," she thought, "all veiled in the mysteries which hide celestial things from human knowing, and all too fragile and beautiful to bear the tarnished glare of earth. So the angels who gave it to me have taken it back to heaven which is its rightful home and there, some day, I shall find it again." As the Woman with the Tired Heart thus brooded, she was conscious of a bright presence hovering above her. The air grew strangely sweet and pure, as though it had just come from some mountain height. She knew then that an angel stood before her, for angels may come and go at will in the Garden of the Soul.

From out of the stillness a voice whispered: "Have you not yet learned that any great and good thing which has been given to earth can never be lost? Your dream of that pure perfect love of soul for soul has unbarred the gates of Heaven, and in the radiance of its light you shall see through the coming years the love in the hearts of men and women becoming a sacred thing. The bestial shall be lifted up to the celestial and the sensual shall be made divine. Even though you must ever go your way alone, your heart shall find its peace in knowing that the ideal which your soul has cherished through the lonely years must one day become *real* in the hearts of humanity."

IMMORTELLES

As the voice ceased speaking the garden grew very still and seemed wrapped in fragrance. Wonderingly the Woman with the Tired Heart opened her eyes and looked around her. The place that had for so long been cold and barren was covered with a wondrous mass of Immortelles, the flower of the soul's awakening.

I think God must have smiled upon the garden.

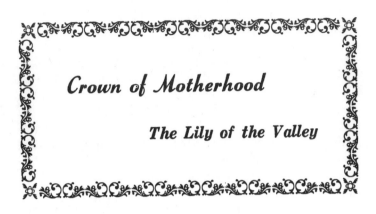

Crown of Motherhood

The Lily of the Valley

"God could not be everywhere and so He made mothers."

One day the great angel Gabriel, who causes all the flowers to grow upon the earth, summoned his angels together and filling their hands and hearts with the sweet peace of heaven, sent them forth to scatter it abroad over the sorrows of the world. He also charged each one to bring to him at the close of the day the most beautiful thing on earth, so that he could transform the loveliest into a rare and perfect flower, and give it back again as an aid and inspiration to earth's children.

Joyously the troop of angels swept away on their gladsome mission, while one who was younger and shyer than the rest loitered far behind. "What shall I ever find," she thought, as she silently floated above the peaceful valleys and the cloud-shadowed hills. "All the world is so beautiful to me."

Swiftly the hours passed and she saw one after another of the angels triumphantly returning to heaven, laden with some fair and wonderful thing each had found upon the earth. One had gathered the pearl mists of dawn; another the dew that sleeps in the heart of a rose. One carried the music that is wafted above a great cathedral; and another had lifted the dreams from a young girl's heart.

As the shadows of evening began to lengthen, the little angel grew disconsolate and her wings drooped wearily

115

above her head; then passing near an open window she suddenly paused and looked in. A young mother was kneeling in rapt adoration above a little bed where a baby lay sleeping. Upon its flower-face, dimpled smiles were playing, and as the angel bent to listen, the mother murmured: "Ah, little love-flower so recently transplanted from the heaven-land, in your slumbers do you not seek again the angel-companions from whom you have been so short a time separated? Bring into my heart some of heaven's own light whereby I may guard and guide you." And as she bent to kiss the smiling face, she whispered reverently: "Dear God, I thank you for that most perfect of all gifts, the Crown of Motherhood."

As she lifted her head, a teardrop sparkling with all the wonder and the glory of a mother's love gleamed upon the brow of the sleeping child. Suddenly there was a soft rush of wings, and the little angel with the tear held close in her heart was joyously returning to her home in heaven.

As she entered the waiting portals, the angel Gabriel was seated upon his great, white throne; and the other angels were gathered all about him.

"Ah, little laggard angel," he chided tenderly, as she came closer, "what is the most beautiful thing that you have brought to me from the earth land?"

Shyly she slipped from her heart the teardrop all weighted with a mother's love. When the angel Gabriel saw it, his face became more beautiful than even the angels had ever seen it before. Reverently he clasped it, and as he held it in his hands, such a halo of light encircled him that all the angels bowed their heads in prayer.

—:—

He was very quiet for a long time and when at last he held out his hands to them it was to say: "The little *Lily of the Valley* is the angels' gift to the mothers of the world."

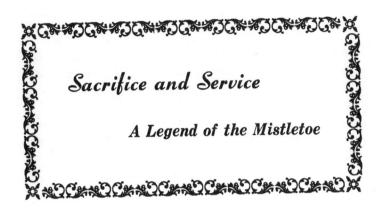

Sacrifice and Service

A Legend of the Mistletoe

All the road
And its rigors
Life and Death
Love's touch transfigures,
And all that lies
In between
Love Sanctifies,
Once the heavenly spark is lighted,
Once in love two hearts united,
Nevermore
Shall aught that was be
As before.

—*Robert Browning*

When the angels return to heaven from their daily work in the world they often recount to one another their experiences. And many times the angel Gabriel, who is their Teacher—for angels learn wonderful things all the time just as earth's children do—often listens to these stories, and sometimes he, too, will tell of the things that he has found in the realm where tears are flowing.

Once as he gathered his angel helpers about him, this is the story that he told them in the twilight time of heaven:

117

A Man and a Woman walked hand in hand for many years upon the earth, and knew a happiness so rare and fine that other mortals had no comprehension of it. One day as they wandered together beneath the shadow of great trees the woman said, "I pray that it may be given us to prove that our love is greater than any that has gone before."

The Man smiled and answered, "That also is the wish that I hold in my heart."

"Here," said the angel Gabriel, "are the two souls that I have searched the world to find." And he caused a picture to form in the Woman's heart in which she saw herself walking alone. And he caused a refrain to sound in the mind of the Man which echoed, "To know the greatest love is to sacrifice personality and work only for the good of the whole."

They looked at each other long and earnestly, and then the Woman questioned anxiously, "Oh tell me, it does not mean that; I can bear anything else!" The Man answered sadly, "It means just that."

They stood silent for a long time and then the Man whispered softly, "Are you strong enough for this?" All the sorrows of the world seemed calling as the Woman murmured sobbingly, "I am."

She clung to him as she whispered sadly, "And you— can you go on alone?" The pain of all the partings that have ever been seemed to fill the silence as the Man answered slowly, "I can."

The ways where they had walked together knew them no more. While a white radiance of the spirit enveloped their work, their human hearts were broken in the sorrow of that parting.

"Have they come to the heaven-worlds?" questioned the angels eagerly, "Let us find and comfort them."

The angel Gabriel smiled understandingly as he replied, "They are not here yet, for they are both young and there is much for them to do in the world of men before they can know a resting time. But look at this," said he, holding out a casket filled with gleaming jewels. "Every day at twilight the Woman, tired and lonely, comes to the shrine of prayer, and there I have gathered some of the tears that fall on her heart; and every day at twilight the Man, footsore and weary, comes to the shrine of prayer, and I have gathered some of the tears that fall on his heart. I keep the tears in this casket, and when the Man and the Woman come to live with us this shall be my gift to welcome them."

"But there are no tears here now," said the angels, "The casket is heaped with pearls that are filled with a wonderful shining."

"Do you not know," said the angel Gabriel, "that those tears were formed of sacrifice and service, the two brightest jewels in the Master's crown? And there are no tears in heaven, when I brought them here they were transformed into jewels like the attributes of which they were formed.

"And now what flower will you give to earth's children to commemorate my story?" asked Gabriel.

The angels gathered around the casket of jewels that seemed to reflect the brightness of their faces and pondered long. When they returned to the angel Gabriel, a mass of pearl-white berries gleamed against their hearts like tears that shine with the tender radiance of a love that is divine.

So the Mistletoe is immortal as ever belonging to lovers.

The Everlasting White Rose

A Legend of the Holy Night

White as an embodied hush;
A very rapture of white;
A wedlock of silence and light,
White, white as the wonder undefiled
Of Eve just wakened in Paradise;
Nay, white as the angel of a child,
That looks into God's own eyes.
　　　　—Harriet McKewen Kimball

Where the portals of time guard the borders of earth from the Unseen land stands the Spirit of Motherhood, gowned in long robes of flowing white that lose themselves in the distance like endless dreams. About her lovely head is wound a misty veil, woven from threads of smiles and tears that cling around her gentle throat as the clasp of tiny hands. Her eyes are lighted beacons gleaming like twin stars of hope. Around her, and far behind, shines a softened light, which is a mere reflection of the love-light in her heart. In her hands she holds a wonderful white rose that seems to be made of a multitude of children's faces. Each soft petal reflects a shining countenance, making an ensemble so enchantingly lovely and so weighted with tenderness that all the weary world grows brighter through its light.

Millions of eager souls who feel the urge to return to

earth life are constantly thronging the portals of Time. Each stands beneath the shadow of the large white rose, and upon each one to whom is granted an opportunity to walk earth-ways again, the Spirit of Motherhood bestows a petal of this rose. For every petal that is removed another comes to take its place. So long as there are souls who yearn for earth experience, so long must the petals continue to bloom. Never withering and never bare, the Everlasting White Rose in all its exquisite mystery dreams above the world.

In the heart of the Holy Night, all of the souls who are to find their earth-homes in the coming year go a-journeying. When all the world is filled with love and every heart is overflowing with peace and good-will, it is very easy for the tenuous bodies of the earth-drawn egos to penetrate into the hearts and homes of their choosing. So on Holy Night a new wave of tenderness encircles each expectant mother; soft hands caress her; flower faces bend over her; and beautiful memories lave her like strains of half-remembered music. The tender fragrance of white rose petals brings her into a newer, and more ethereal consciousness. Ah, the exquisite happiness that beckons her on this Holiest Night for mothers, while the angels sing of the coming of The Child.

—:—

Along an interminable skyline rest shadows of lavender-grey clouds; here and there the bright face of a star may be seen. A silver sheen of mist shrouds all things, with only an occasional splash of mauve light glancing through to herald the approaching dawn. The soft mist stirs gently like a curtain to and fro, opening tender arms to welcome the return of the tiny souls from their love-journeyings. Thousands of happy cherubs, their faces shining with a moonlit radiance, slip behind the silver mists to await their Star-call in the coming year.

NEW AGE WRITINGS BY CORINNE HELINE

New Age Bible Interpretation

Old Testament
Vol I   - Five Books of Moses and Joshua
Vol II - Part I. Solomon and the Temple Builders
          Part II. Books of Initiation
Vol III - Part I. The Promise
          Part II. The Preparation

New Testament
Vol IV. Preparation for coming of the Light of the World
Vol V. The Christ and His Mission
Vol VI. The Work of the Apostles and Paul and Book of Revelation
Vol VII Mystery of the Christos
Other Books on Bible Interpretation

Tarot and the Bible - Mythology and the Bible - Mystic Masonry and the Bible - Occult Anatomy and the Bible - The Bible and the Stars - Sacred Science of Numbers - Questions and Answers on Bible Enigmas   Supreme Initiations of the Blessed Virgin.

Other Works

Magic Gardens - Star Gates - Color and Music in the New Age - Music: the Keynote of Human Evolution - The Cosmic Harp - Healing and Regeneration through Color - Healing and Regeneration through Music - Esoteric Music of Richard Wagner - Beethoven's Nine Symphonies - The Twelve Labors of Hercules - Mysteries of the Holy Grail

NEW AGE WRITINGS BY THEODORE HELINE

America's Destiny, The American Indian, The Archetype Unveiled - Capital Punishment - Esoteric Drama Studies - Romeo and Juliet - The Merchant of Venice - Saint Francis and the Wolf of Gubbio

• •

A current price list may be obtained from

New Age Bible and Philosophy Center
1139 Lincoln Boulevard
Santa Monica, California 90403

Telephone (213) 395-4346

Cover painting by: Ruth Harwood